A Handknit Romance

A Handknit Romance

22 Vintage Designs with Lovely Details

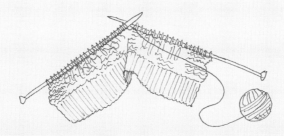

JENNIE ATKINSON

Photography by Nick Sargeant

INTERWEAVE PRESS

www.interweave.com

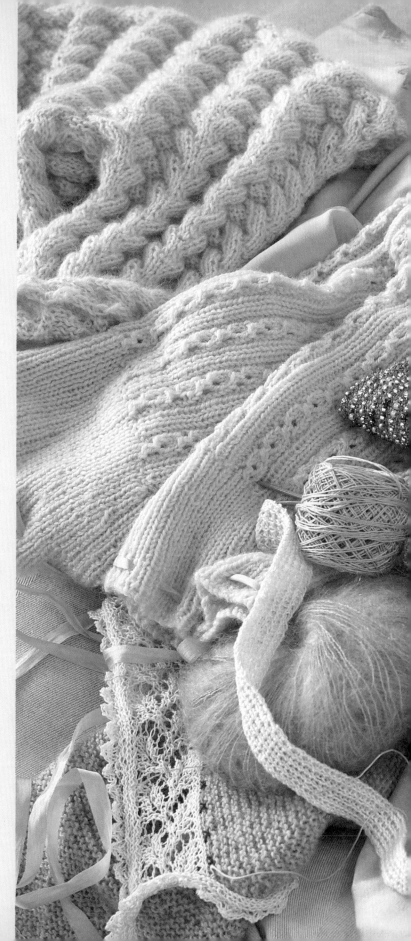

A Handknit Romance

First published in the United States by
Interweave Press LLC
201 East Fourth St.
Loveland, CO 80537
interweave.com

First published in the United Kingdom in 2011 by
Berry & Bridges Ltd
Suite 416, Belsize Business Centre
258 Belsize Road
London NW6 4BT

Editor Katie Hardwicke
Designer Anne Wilson
Styling and Illustrations Jennie Atkinson
Pattern writers Sue Whiting and Sarah Hatton
Technical editor Therese Chynoweth
Pattern diagrams Therese Chynoweth
Charts Lisa Richardson and Therese Chynoweth

Publisher Susan Berry

ISBN 978-1-59668-779-0

Library of Congress Cataloging-in-Publication
data not available at time of publication.

Reproduced and printed in Singapore

Contents

Introduction

I love looking around vintage fashion fairs and marvelling at the seemingly endless variety of wonderful fabrics, colors, and textures that make up the garments and accessories found there. My particular favorites are the pieces that originate in the decades of the

early 20th century: the peachy satins and softly-draping crepes of the 1930s; the glistening sequins and sparkling crystal beads of the 1920s; crisp white Victorian cottons; and the delicately embroidered and pintucked fine cotton-lawns of the Edwardian era. Hours of careful handwork went into making some of these garments, and creative techniques for decoration and texture abound: minute embroidery stitches and delicate beadwork; finely worked knitting and crochet; intricate cobweb lace. And this creativity is not restricted to garments, but is also found in a wonderfully inventive array of purses, bags, hats, shawls, gloves, and trimmings. Even underwear, rarely seen by anyone but the wearer, was

beautifully hand-sewn with tiny stitches in an era when the greatest care was taken in making items meant to last a lifetime. The fact that these treasures have survived fairly intact for so many years is testament to their amazing quality.

The garments and accessories in this book have been inspired by the colors and textures of these vintage pieces, and by their style, details, and delicacy.

Sadly, very few vintage hand-knitted garments have survived, but my favorite aspect of the ones that have is that they actually look handmade. One reason for this is because they were often knitted loosely in fine yarn, resulting in a slightly uneven gauge. I love this slight imperfection, as I believe it is this that makes handmade items unique and beautiful. I have chosen to use fine yarns for the pieces included here, as it gives a delicacy that cannot be achieved with heavier yarns, and also allows for far more detail, and if this results in a handmade quality or finish, then so much the better.

I realize fine yarns mean the pieces will take longer to knit, and therefore demand more commitment from the knitter—but I really think it is worth it to achieve the same precious quality found in vintage clothing.

All the sample garments for the book were knitted by me, so I can vouch for the fact that none is very difficult to make—although some require more patience than others! Accessories, such as gloves and scarves, are included for those knitters who like to achieve quicker results with smaller items.

Making your projects unique

One of the most exciting aspects of knitting is the fact that the knitter can choose between stitch, yarn, color, and any combination of these and therefore create unique pieces. Add

to this the fact that beads can be knitted-in, or embroidery worked on the finished piece—and the possibilities are endless.

When conceiving this book, my aim was not just to recreate vintage style in knit, but also to encourage knitters to use the creative finishes shown on the clothing and accessories of past eras.

Nowadays, the fact that many knitters like to personalize existing patterns with their own choice of yarns and colors has

been demonstrated through the internet on knitters' networking sites such as Ravelry, and in the many knitting magazines where knitters post images of their work. The internet has played a major role in the steadily growing popularity of knitting, and the huge variety of yarns readily available from around the world mean there is an endless choice for the creative knitter.

With both these points in mind, I hope readers of this book will feel inspired to interpret the designs here in their own way; substituting yarns, colors, decoration, and finishes, thereby making the items they knit very personal and totally unique. As long as the yarn gauge matches that of the pattern shown, there is no reason why an adventurous knitter cannot be highly inventive—there really are no limits to what you can produce!

Customizing the designs

Here are some handy tips and suggestions to help you when knitting the designs to find ways to give them your own unique interpretation.

CHOOSING YARN SUBSTITUTES

When planning a garment design, the type of yarn chosen makes all the difference to the way the garment looks. I often knit swatches in a variety of stitches to see what works best for that yarn. For a garment that needs to have some "give" or elasticity so that it fits well—like the Lace stockings (page 56)—I would choose a springy pure wool that allows the stockings to cling to the leg and also keeps its shape. Whereas for a loose garment where drape is the most important factor, such as the Beaded top (page 64), a yarn which has no elasticity but hangs well, like the Bamboo yarn I chose, is ideal. So, when making a substitution, think about matching the character of the yarn as well as the weight. If you knitted the stockings in the bamboo yarn the textured stitch would look flat and the stockings would be baggy. If you knitted the beaded top in a springier wool yarn, it would lose its elegant drape.

There are so many different yarn types available now that it is impossible to generalize, but as a rough guide, wool, wool mixes, and synthetic wool substitutes are the yarns that have most elasticity, and these are great for knitting plain and textured stitches and for garments that fit. Yarns that have no stretch are good for draped garments or knitting lace stitches.

When substituting yarns, always knit a swatch first in the chosen yarn, not only to check that it has the same gauge but also to check that the "feel" of the yarn is suitable for the design.

Gauge and yarn quantities

When substituting yarn it is best to find a replacement with exactly the same gauge/needle size as the suggested yarn, but you can usually change the needle size up or down by one or two sizes to give the right gauge without affecting the way the knitting handles. Be aware that even slight variations in the gauge will affect the final size. Remember that a yarn that has more stitches to the inch than the suggested yarn is thinner, so knitting in

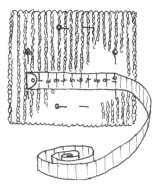

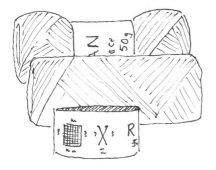

this yarn would make the piece smaller, alternatively if the substitute yarn has fewer stitches to the inch, it is thicker and would make a bigger piece of knitting.

Finally, to work out how much of the substitute yarn you will need, look at the yardage given for a ball of the suggested yarn, not just the ball weight, as some fibers are denser than others. For example, a 1¾ oz (50 g) ball of 4-ply cotton might have 153 yd (140 m), and a 1¾ oz (50 g) ball of 4-ply wool might have 174 yd (160 m), even though they are both described as 4-ply and have the same stitch gauge.

You therefore need to calculate how many balls of the substitute yarn are required based on the yardage per ball. Multiply the length of the yarn suggested in the pattern by the number of balls needed for your size. Then divide the result by the length given for a ball of your substitute yarn.

Here is an example: to change the cotton yarn in the Fitted jacket (page 12) to a wool yarn, for bust size 34", the pattern states you need 11 balls of cotton with 153 yd per ball. Multiply the number of balls by yardage: 11 x 153 = 1683 yd.

If the substitute wool yarn has 174 yd per ball, divide 1683 by 174 = 10 balls. This is the number of balls of replacement wool yarn required.

Ideas for yarn substitutions
- Fitted jacket (page 12) and Cotton skirt (page 20)— These would both work very well in similar weight wool yarn.
- Lurex dress (page116)— This could be knitted in a similar weight plain yarn instead, but choose a yarn that has a drape— such as linen or silk— for the best match.
- Lace scarf (page 112)— This could be knitted in lurex yarn to make it a lovely accessory for evening wear.

CHANGING COLOR
Another way to give a garment a completely different look is through the choice of color. Obviously this could be a straightforward color swap, but it could also involve the creative use of color combinations in a single garment.

Ideas for color changes
- Fitted jacket (page 12)—Instead of making crochet buttons, you could purchase contrast colored buttons. Or, if you are feeling more adventurous, the cuffs, collar, and rever button band facings could be knitted in a contrast color.
- Wrapover cardigan (page 40)—The ribs and the crossover ties could be knitted in a contrast color.

• Beaded top (page 64)—This would look great in black, or a rich, dark color, with silver beads. Or, equally dramatic, a bright color (vibrant red or clear blue) with either black or white beads.

• Cotton camisole (page 26), Lace-edged camisole (page 50), Sailor-collar blouse (page 96), or Lace blouse (page 80)—Using a contrast color for the lace or crochet edgings would give a different look to all these garments.

HAND FINISHES

Hand embroidery on knitwear is very simple and quick to do, and can be really effective. A few of the most basic embroidery stitches, such as cross stitch and herringbone stitch, and French and bullion knots, are illustrated in this book (see pages 55 and 35). Try them on different garments to the ones shown.

Suggestions for embroidery

• The cross stitch shown on the Lace-edged camisole (page 50) would look lovely worked in cream cotton around the

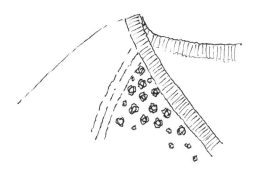

stockinette stitch band at the neck of the Cotton camisole (page 26) to match the color of the buttons and ribbon.

• The bullion stitch flower design of the Heart lavender bags (page 36) could be worked on the Wrapover cardigan (page 40) at the neck as a "corsage."

• For understated embellishment, you could decorate the crochet buttons on the Fitted jacket (page 12) with simple embroidery.

CREATING A VINTAGE LOOK

Attractive or unusual buttons and beads can be saved from old garments, jewelry, or accessories and given a new lease of life on your knitting projects.

Suggestions for vintage-style trims

• The Beaded bag (page 76) and Beaded purse (page 130) have recycled frames from second-hand bags found in vintage markets. Check first that the frame has the holes around it that allow you to sew the knitted fabric to it. It is easy to change the size of your knitted piece to match the frame by adding or subtracting a few stitches. This is a great

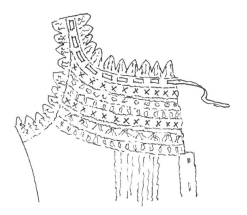

way to recycle lovely frames and give an authentic vintage look to your bag.

• The Crochet necklace (page 46) was made from a lovely—but broken—vintage necklace, that was lying unused in a jewelry box. Check that the beads you wish to reuse have a hole large enough to thread the yarn through.

Creating your own vintage-style trims

• If the ribbon you buy for the Cotton camisole (page 26) or the Heart lavender bags (page 36) looks too new for your lovely vintage-style items, you can give it an aged look by tea-dyeing it. Simply dip the ribbon into a cup of srong tea and leave it to soak (experiment with the strength of the solution and the timing first on a short length of ribbon, as you don't want your ribbon to be too orange).

• Tea-dyeing is a great way to give a vintage look to new items and white cotton can be similarly dyed to give it an antique look. Once the item has reached the chosen shade, remove it, rinse it in clean water, and let dry. If it is too light in shade, repeat the process.

ADAPTING GARMENT STYLES

Most of the garments in the book are simple shapes that can be adapted to suit the individual knitter.

Suggestions

• Knit the Lurex dress (page116) in a single color, perhaps with fewer lace pattern repeats to make it shorter, and pulled in at the waist with the tie belt, to make a great tunic instead. It could be worn over wide, soft palazzo pants, or even leggings. The same treatment would also work for the Flapper dress (page 124).

• You could make the Wrapover cardigan (page 40) without the ties, fastening it instead with a button and loop or pretty brooch.

• Make the Lace scarf (page 112) longer and wear it as a shawl, or match with the Openwork gloves (page 106) by knitting the scarf in the same color as the contrast edging of the gloves for a pretty and sophisticated accessory set.

Fitted jacket

Victorian women were never without their corsets, which gave them their exaggerated hourglass figures. This jacket, knitted in 4-ply mercerized cotton, is inspired by that look, with shaping accentuating the waist, and a flared "bustle" at the back. It has puffed three-quarter length sleeves, a rever collar and cuffs, and large crochet buttons that give the jacket an authentic vintage feel.

For this design, I have used a particular form of shaping, known as short-row shaping, to achieve the fullness. The buttons draw attention to the waist.

Jacket inspiration

The inspiration for this fitted jacket comes from the elegantly shaped dresses of the late Victorian period, with their narrow waist and gathered fullness at the back.

FINISHED SIZE

To fit bust 32 (34, 36, 38, 40, 42)" (81.5 [86.5, 91.5, 96.5, 101.5, 106.5] cm).
Finished length 20¾ (21½, 21½, 22½, 22½, 23½)" (53 [55, 55, 57, 57, 60] cm).

YARN

Rowan "Siena 4-ply" (100% cotton, 153 yd [140 m]/50 g): mauve (Floret 658), 13 (13, 14, 14, 14, 15) balls.

NEEDLES AND CROCHET HOOK

U.S. size 2/3 (3 mm) needles; U.S. size 2 (2.75 mm) needles; U.S. size 5 (3.75 mm) needles; U.S. size C-2 (2.75 mm) crochet hook. Adjust needle size if necessary to obtain correct gauge.

NOTIONS

Stitch holder; markers (m).

GAUGE

28 stitches and 37 rows = 4" (10 cm) in stockinette stitch.

ABBREVIATIONS

See page 133.
Crochet instructions use U.S. terms, see page 133 for U.K. equivalents.

BACK

Using U.S. size 2/3 (3 mm) needles, CO 218 (226, 232, 238, 246, 252) sts.
Knit 4 rows.
Beg with a RS row, work 6 rows in St st.

Bustle shaping

Next row K41 (45, 48, 51, 55, 58), skp, [k2tog, k18, sl 1, k1, psso] 6 times, k2tog, k41 (45, 48, 51, 55, 58)— 204 (212, 218, 224, 232, 238) sts.
Work 5 rows in St st.

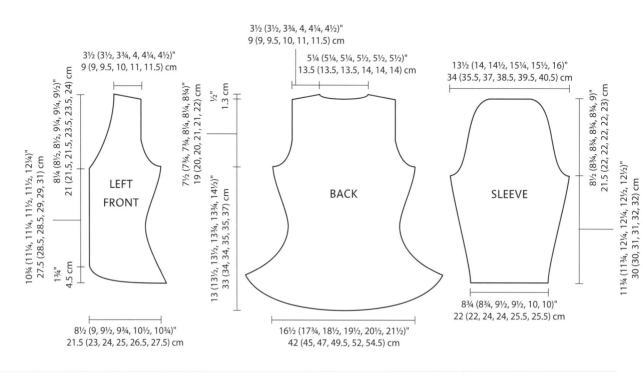

LEFT FRONT

3½ (3½, 3¾, 4, 4¼, 4½)"
9 (9, 9.5, 10, 11, 11.5) cm

10¾ (11¼, 11¼, 11½, 11½, 12¼)"
27.5 (28.5, 28.5, 29, 29, 31) cm

8¼ (8½, 8½, 9¼, 9¼, 9½)"
21 (21.5, 21.5, 23.5, 23.5, 24) cm

1¾"
4.5 cm

8½ (9, 9½, 9¾, 10½, 10¾)"
21.5 (23, 24, 25, 26.5, 27.5) cm

BACK

3½ (3½, 3¾, 4, 4¼, 4½)"
9 (9, 9.5, 10, 11, 11.5) cm

5¼ (5¼, 5¼, 5½, 5½, 5½)"
13.5 (13.5, 13.5, 14, 14, 14) cm

½"
1.3 cm

7½ (7¾, 7¾, 8¼, 8¼, 8¾)"
19 (20, 20, 21, 21, 22) cm

13 (13½, 13½, 13¾, 13¾, 14½)"
33 (34, 34, 35, 35, 37) cm

16½ (17¾, 18½, 19½, 20½, 21½)"
42 (45, 47, 49.5, 52, 54.5) cm

SLEEVE

13½ (14, 14½, 15¼, 15½, 16)"
34 (35.5, 37, 38.5, 39.5, 40.5) cm

8½ (8¾, 8¾, 8¾, 8¾, 9)"
21.5 (22, 22, 22, 22, 23) cm

11¾ (11¾, 12¼, 12¼, 12½, 12½)"
30 (30, 31, 31, 32, 32) cm

8¾ (8¾, 9½, 9½, 10, 10)"
22 (22, 24, 24, 25.5, 25.5) cm

Next row K40 (44, 47, 50, 54, 57), skp, [k2tog, k16, skp] 6 times, k2tog, k40 (44, 47, 50, 54, 57)—190 (198, 204, 210, 218, 224) sts.

Work 5 rows in St st.

These 12 rows set bustle decreases.

Dec as set on next row, then every 6th row **AT SAME TIME**, shaping Back by dec 1st at both ends of 19th, then every 18th row until the foll row has been worked:

K2tog, k29 (33, 36, 39, 43, 46), skp, [k2tog, k2, skp] 6 times, k2tog, k29 (33, 36, 39, 43, 46), k2tog—86 (94, 100, 106, 114, 120) sts.

Work 5 rows in St st.

Next row (inc row) K31 (35, 38, 41, 45, 48), M1, k24, M1, k31 (35, 38, 41, 45, 48)—88 (96, 102, 108, 116, 122) sts.

Work 5 rows in St st.

Next row Inc in first st, k30 (34, 37, 40, 44, 47), M1, k26, M1, k30 (34, 37, 40, 44, 47), inc in last st—92 (100, 106, 112, 120, 126) sts.

Cont to M1 at waist of every 6th row and **AT SAME TIME** 1 st at each end of every 12th row until the foll row has been worked:

Inc in first st, k34 (38, 41, 44, 48, 51) M1, k42, M1, k34 (38, 41, 44, 48, 51), inc in last st—116 (124, 130, 136, 144, 150) sts.

Cont without shaping until work measures 13 (13½, 13½, 14, 14, 14½)" (33 [34.5, 34.5, 35.5, 35.5, 37] cm), ending with a WS row.

Shape armholes

BO 4 (5, 5, 6, 6, 7) sts at beg of next 2 rows— 108 (114, 120, 124, 132, 136) sts.

BO 2 (3, 3, 2, 3, 3) sts at beg of next 2 rows— 104 (108, 114, 120, 126, 130) sts.

BO 2 sts at beg of next 2 rows— 100 (104, 110, 116, 122, 126) sts.

Dec 1 st at each end of next row, every other row 4 (5, 6, 7, 8, 8) times, then every 4th row 3 times—84 (86, 90, 94, 98, 102) sts.

Cont without shaping until armhole measures

7½ (8, 8, 8½, 8½, 8¾)" (19 [20.5, 20.5, 21.5, 21.5, 22] cm), ending with a WS row.

Shoulders and Neck shaping

Next row (RS) BO 8 (8, 9, 9, 10, 11) sts, k18 (19, 20, 21, 22, 23), turn.

Next row P2tog, purl to end—17 (18, 19, 20, 21, 22) sts.

Next row BO 8 (8, 9, 9, 10, 11) sts, knit to last 2 sts, k2tog—8 (9, 9, 10, 10, 10) sts.

Next row Purl.

BO rem sts.

With RS tog, rejoin yarn to rem sts, BO center 32 (32, 32, 34, 34, 34) sts for Back Neck, knit to end —26 (27, 29, 30, 32, 34) sts.

Complete to match first side of neck, reversing all shaping.

LEFT FRONT

Using U.S. size 2/3 (3 mm) needles, CO 65 (69, 72, 75, 79, 82) sts.

Knit 4 rows.

Shape front edge

Row 1 (RS) K53 (57, 60, 63, 67, 70), turn and purl to end.

Row 3 K55 (59, 62, 65, 69, 72), turn and purl to end.

Row 5 K57 (61, 64, 67, 71, 74), turn and purl to end.

Row 7 K35 (39, 42, 45, 49, 52), skp, k2tog, k20, turn, and purl to end—63 (67, 70, 73, 77, 80) sts.

Row 9 K59 (63, 66, 69, 73, 76), turn, and purl to end.

Row 11 K61 (65, 68, 71, 75, 78), turn, and purl to end.

Row 13 K34 (38, 41, 44, 48, 51), skp, k2tog, knit to end—61 (65, 68, 71, 75, 78) sts.

Cont to dec as set on every 6th row 7 more times and **AT SAME TIME** dec 1 st at beg of 6th and then every 18th row until the foll row has been worked:

Next row K2tog, k23 (27, 30, 33, 37, 40), skp, k2tog, k18—44 (48, 51, 54, 58, 61) sts.

Work 5 rows in St st.

Next row (inc row) K25 (29, 32, 35, 39, 42), M1, k19—45 (49, 52, 55, 59, 62) sts.

Work 5 rows in St st.

Next row Inc in first st, k24 (28, 31, 34, 38, 41), M1, k20—47 (51, 54, 57, 61, 64) sts.

Work 5 rows in St st.

Next row K26 (30, 33, 36, 40, 43), M1, k21—48 (52, 55, 58, 62, 65) sts.

Cont to M1 at waist of every 6th row and **AT SAME TIME** inc 1 st as set at beg of 6th row, then every 12th row until the foll row has been worked:

Next row Inc in first st, k28 (32, 35, 38, 42, 45) M1, k28—59 (63, 66, 69, 73, 76) sts.

Cont in St st without shaping until 4 fewer rows have been worked than on back to start of armhole shaping, ending with a WS row.

Front Neck shaping

Next row (RS) Knit to last 4 sts, k2tog, k2— 1 st dec'd.

Next row Purl.

Rep these 2 rows once, ending with a WS row—57 (61, 64, 67, 71, 74) sts.

(Work should now match back to start of armhole shaping.)

Shape armhole

Next row BO 4 (5, 5, 6, 6, 7) sts, knit to last 4 sts, k2tog, k2—52 (55, 58, 60, 64, 66) sts.

Work 1 row.

Next row BO 2 (3, 3, 2, 3, 3) sts, knit to last 4 sts, k2tog, k2—49 (51, 54, 57, 60, 62) sts.

Work 1 row.

Next row BO 2 sts, knit to last 4 sts, k2tog, k2—46 (48, 51, 54, 57, 59) sts.

Work 1 row.

Dec 1 st at beg of next and every other row 4 (5, 6, 7, 8, 8) times, then every 4th row 3 times and **AT SAME TIME** dec 1 st at neck edge as set at end of every RS row twice, every 4th row 7 times, then every 6th row 5 (6, 5, 6, 6, 6) times—24 (24, 27, 28, 30, 32) sts.

Cont until armhole matches back to start of shoulder, ending with a WS row.

BO 8 (8, 9, 9, 10, 11) sts at beg of next 2 RS rows.

Work 1 row.

BO rem sts.

RIGHT FRONT

Using U.S. size 2/3 (3 mm) needles, CO 65 (69, 72, 75, 79, 82) sts.

Knit 5 rows.

Shape front edge

Row 1 (WS) P53 (57, 60,63, 67, 70), turn, and knit to end.

Row 3 P55 (59, 62, 65, 69, 72), turn, and knit to end.

Row 5 P57 (61, 64, 67, 71, 74), turn.

Row 6 K18, skp, k2tog, knit to end—63 (67, 70, 73, 77, 80) sts.

Row 7 P59 (63, 66, 69, 73, 76), turn, and knit to end.

Complete as given for Left Front, reversing all shaping.

For example, the neck shaping will be worked as k2, skp, knit to end.

SLEEVES (Make 2)

Using U.S. size 2/3 (3 mm) needles, CO 62 (62, 66, 66, 70, 70) sts.

Beg with a RS row and working in St st throughout, inc 1 st at each end of 9th row, every 4th row 0 (4, 4, 10, 6, 12) times, then every 6th row 15 (13, 13, 9, 12, 8) times—94 (98, 102, 106, 108, 112) sts.

Cont without shaping until sleeve measures 12

(12, 12¼, 12¼, 12½, 12½)" (30.5 [30.5, 31, 31, 32, 32] cm) ending with a WS row.

Shape sleeve cap

BO 4 (5, 5, 6, 6, 7) sts at beg of next 2 rows—86 (88, 92, 94, 96, 98) sts.

BO 2 (3, 3, 2, 3, 3) sts at beg of next 2 rows—82 (82, 86, 90, 90, 92) sts.

BO 2 sts at beg of next 2 rows—78 (78, 82, 86, 86, 88) sts.

Dec 1 st at each end of next row, then every other row 1 (1, 1, 3, 3, 3) time(s), every 6th row 4 (5, 1, 0, 0, 0) time(s), every 4th row 6 (5, 11, 12, 12, 12) times, then every other row 2 (2, 2, 2, 3) times—50 sts.

Work 1 row, ending with a WS row.

BO 4 sts at beg of next 4 rows.

BO rem 34 sts.

CUFFS (Make 2)

Using U.S. size 2/3 (3 mm) needles, CO 82 (82, 86, 86, 70, 70) sts.

Knit 4 rows.

Next row Knit.

Next row K4, purl to last 4 sts, k4.

Rep last 2 rows 15 times.

BO.

COLLAR (Make 2—1 for facing)

Using U.S. size 2 (2.75 mm) needles, CO 118 (118, 118, 122, 122, 122) sts.

Knit 4 rows.

Next row Knit.

Next row K4, purl to last 4 sts, k4.

Rep these 2 rows until collar measures 4" (10 cm), ending with a WS row.

BO 4 sts at beg of next 4 rows—102 (102, 102, 106, 106, 106) sts.

BO 8 sts at beg of next 4 rows—70 (70, 70, 74, 74, 74) sts.

BO 10 sts at beg of next 4 rows—30 (30, 30, 34, 34, 34) sts.

BO rem sts.

LEFT BUTTON BAND AND REVER COLLAR

Pm at front neck 6 (6, 6, 6¼, 6¼, 6¼)" (15 [15, 15, 16, 16, 16] cm) down from shoulder on both sides of front.

With RS tog, using U.S. size 2 (2.75 mm) needles, pick up and knit 20 (24, 24, 24, 24, 26) sts from neck marker down to beg of neck shaping, then 76 (74, 74, 78, 78, 80) sts down left front edge to bottom of garter st edge—96 (98, 98, 102, 102, 106) sts.

Knit 3 rows.

Rows 4 and 5 (RS) (shaping rever collar) K27 (31, 31, 31, 31, 33) sts, pm on needle, turn and wrap next st to prevent hole, purl to last 3 sts, k3.

Row 6 Knit to end.

Row 7 K3, purl to last 3sts, M1, k3—97 (99, 99, 103, 103, 107) sts.

Rep Rows 4 to 7 once more, working Row 4 to marker on needle—98 (100, 100, 104, 104, 108) sts.

Rep Rows 4 to 6 once more, working Row 4 to marker on needle.

Row 15 K3, purl to marker, (p5 [6, 6, 6, 6, 6], M1) 5 times, p1 (0, 0, 0, 0, 2), k3—103 (105, 105, 109, 109, 113) sts.

Rep Rows 4 to 7 twice, then Rows 4 to 6 once more, working Row 4 to marker on needle—105 (107, 107, 111, 111, 115) sts.

Row 27 K3, purl to marker (p7 [7, 7, 7, 7, 7], M1) 4 times, purl to last 3 sts, M1, k3—110 (112, 112, 116, 116, 120) sts.

Row 28 K37 (41, 41, 41, 41, 43), wrap next st and turn.

Row 29 Purl to last 3 sts, k3.

Row 30 K33 (37, 37, 37, 37, 39), wrap next st and turn.

Row 31 Purl to last 3 sts, M1, k3—111 (113, 113, 117, 117, 121) sts.

Row 32 K30 (34, 34, 34, 34, 36), wrap next st and turn.

Row 33 Purl to last 3 sts, k3.

Row 34 K26 (30, 30, 30, 30, 32), wrap next st and turn.

Row 35 Purl to last 3 sts, M1, k3—112 (114, 114, 118, 118, 122) sts.

Row 36 K23 (27, 27, 27, 27, 29), wrap next st and turn.

Row 37 Purl to last 3 sts, k3.

Row 38 Knit to end.

Knit 4 rows.

(WS) BO using U.S. size 5 (3.75 mm) needles.

RIGHT BUTTON BAND AND REVER COLLAR

With RS tog and U.S. size 2 (2.75 mm) needles, pick up and knit 76 (74, 74, 78, 78, 80) sts up Right Front edge to beg of neck shaping, then 20 (24, 24, 24, 24, 26) sts from neck shaping to marker—96 (98, 98, 102, 102, 106) sts.

Knit 4 rows.

Rows 5 and 6 (WS) K3, p24 (28, 28, 28, 28, 30) sts, pm on needle, turn, and knit all sts.

Row 7 K3, purl to last 3 sts, k3.

Row 8 Knit to last 3 sts, M1, k3—97 (99, 99, 103, 103, 107) sts.

Rep Rows 5 to 8 once, then rep Rows 5 and 6 once more—98 (100, 100, 104, 104, 108) sts.

Row 15 K3, p1 (0, 0, 0, 0, 2), [M1, p5 (6, 6, 6, 6, 6)] 5 times, purl to last 3 sts, k3—103 (105, 105, 109, 109, 113) sts.

Row 16 Rep Row 8—104 (106, 106, 110, 100, 114) sts.

Row 17 Rep Row 5.

Row 18 Rep Row 6.

Row 19 (button band row) K3, purl to 5 (3, 3, 4, 4, 3) sts past marker, [BO 7 sts, p11 (11, 11, 12, 12, 13)] 3 times, BO 7 sts, k3.

Row 20 Knit, casting on over BO sts of last row. Complete to match Left Button Band and Collar, reversing all shaping.

Left Band Facing

Using U.S. size 2 (2.75mm) needles, CO 96 (98, 98, 102, 102, 106) sts and complete to match Right Button Band and Collar without buttonholes.

Right Band Facing

Using U.S. size 2 (2.75 mm) needles, CO 96 (98, 98, 102, 102, 106) sts and complete to match Left Button band and Collar, working buttonhole on Row 18 as foll:

Next row Knit to 5 (3, 3, 4, 4, 3) sts past marker, [BO 7, k11 (11, 11, 12, 12, 13)] 3 times, BO 7, k3.

FINISHING

Join shoulder and side seams.

Sew collar and collar facing together with WS of work facing.

Sew BO edge of collar to neck between revers, with seam on right side of garment, and easing at back neck. Join end of collar to top edge of rever for approx 1" (2.5 cm) from neck seam. Sew facings to inside of Front Bands.

Match up buttonholes on band and facing, and sew together around buttonhole.

Join sleeve seams. Fold sleeve in half at cuff, and mark point opposite to seam.

Sew cuffs to end of sleeves so cuff overlaps by 1" (2.5 cm) at marked point.

Mark sleeve cap at both edges about 2" (5 cm) down from BO edge. Sew sleeve into armhole, easing at top edge between these marks to give puff effect.

CROCHET BUTTONS (Make 8)

Using U.S. size C-2 (2.75 mm) crochet hook, ch 2.

Rnd 1 Work 6 sc into 2nd ch from hook, slip st into 1 st chain.

Rnd 2 Ch 1, work 2 sc into each sc of last round (12 sts), ss into first sc.

Rnd 3 Ch 1, * work 1 sc into each of first 2 sc,

then 2 sc into 3rd, rep from * to end of rnd (16 sts), slip st into first sc.

Rnd 4 Ch 1, * work 1 sc into each of first 3 sc, then 2 sc into 4th, rep from * to end (20 sts), slip st into first sc.

Rnd 5 Rep last rnd— 25 sts.

Rnd 6 Ch 1, * work 1 sc into each of first 4 sc, then 2 sc into 5th, rep from * to end— 30 sts.

Rnd 7 Ch 1, * work 1 sc into each of first 5 sc, then skip next sc, rep from * to end— 25 sts.

Rnd 8 Ch 1, * work 1 sc into each of first 4 sc, then skip next sc, rep from * to end— 20 sts.

Rnd 9 Rep last rnd— 16 sts.

Rnd 10 Ch 1, * work 1 sc into each of first 3 sc, then skip next sc, rep from * to end— 12 sts.

Rnd 11 Ch 1, * work 1 sc into each of first 2 sc, then skip next sc, rep from * to end— 8 sts.

Cut yarn leaving end long enough to sew to jacket, and fasten off.

Sew buttons to Front, Cuffs, and at Back as shown.

CHAIN

Using U.S. size C-2 (2.75 mm) crochet hook, make a chain 30" (76 cm) long to wind in figure 8 around both back buttons to fit.

Cotton skirt

Very few vintage knitted items survive, but you can occasionally find original 19th-century knitted petticoats in vintage fairs and markets. The originals were knitted in fine white cotton and were full in shape (to suit the skirts and dresses of the period). My version turns it into an attractive skirt, knitted in sections, starting with the bottom pleated border, in a more manageable 3-ply crochet cotton. The ribbed yoke and drawstring allows you to vary the length by wearing on the waist or the hip. It looks great worn over a vintage cotton lacy petticoat, as here.

Skirt inspiration

Fine handknits were popular in the 19th century, both for underwear and for children's garments. The inspiration for this skirt can be found in the hand-knitted petticoats and children's dresses of the period, like this one, with its ribbed body and full skirt patterned in bands of different lace stitches.

FINISHED SIZE

To fit hips 34 (36, 38, 40, 42, 44)" (86.5 [91.5, 96.5, 101.5, 106.5, 112] cm).

Finished length (from waist tie) 24¾ (25, 25½, 26, 26¼, 26¾)" (63 [63.5, 65, 66, 66.5, 68] cm).

YARN

Size 5 pearl cotton:

DMC "Petra 5" (100% cotton, 437 yd [400 m]/100 g): navy (5823), 4 (5, 5, 5, 6, 6) balls.

NEEDLES AND CROCHET HOOK

U.S. size 2 (2.75 mm) needles: one pair straight needles and 24" (60 cm) circular (circ) needle; U.S. size D-3 (3 mm) crochet hook. Adjust needle size if necessary to obtain correct gauge.

NOTIONS

Markers (m).

GAUGE

32 stitches and 40 rows = 4" (10 cm) in stockinette stitch.

ABBREVIATIONS

See page 133.

Crochet instructions use U.S. terms, see page 133 for U.K. equivalents.

LACE BORDER

CO 38 sts.

Row 1 K6, k2tog, k2, [yo, k2tog] twice, yo, k1, yo, k2, k2tog, k4, k2tog, k2, [yo, k2tog] twice, yo, k1, yo, k2, k2tog, k2.

Row 2 and every foll alt row K2, purl to last st, k1.

Row 3 K1, [k2tog, k2] twice, [yo, k2tog] twice, yo, k3, yo, [k2, k2tog] twice, k2, [yo, k2tog] twice, [yo, k3] twice, k2.

Row 5 K1, [k2tog] twice, k2, [yo, k2tog] twice,

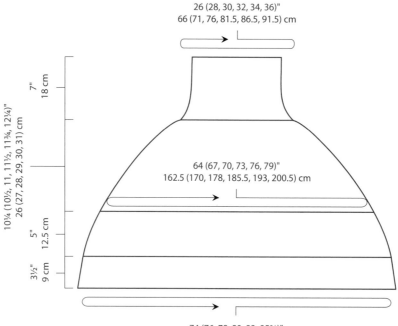

26 (28, 30, 32, 34, 36)"
66 (71, 76, 81.5, 86.5, 91.5) cm

7"
18 cm

10¼ (10½, 11, 11½, 11¾, 12¼)"
26 (27, 28, 29, 30, 31) cm

64 (67, 70, 73, 76, 79)"
162.5 (170, 178, 185.5, 193, 200.5) cm

5"
12.5 cm

3½"
9 cm

74 (76, 78, 80, 82, 85¾)"
188 (193, 198, 203, 208, 218) cms

yo, k5, yo, k2, [k2tog] twice, k2, [yo, k2tog] twice, [yo, k5] twice.

Row 7 K1, k2tog, k2, yo, k1, [yo, k2tog] twice, yo, k2, k2tog, k4, k2tog, k2, yo, k1, [yo, k2tog] twice, yo, k2, k2tog, k7.

Row 9 K4, yo, k3, [yo, k2tog] twice, yo, [k2, k2tog] twice, k2, yo, k3, [yo, k2tog] twice, yo, [k2, k2tog] twice, k2.

Row 11 K4, yo, k5, [yo, k2tog] twice, yo, k2, [k2tog] twice, k2, yo, k5, [yo, k2tog] twice, yo, k2, [k2tog] twice, k2.

Row 12 As Row 2.

These 12 rows form patt.

Cont in patt until lace border measures 74 (76, 78, 80, 82, 86)" (188 [193, 198, 203, 208, 218.5] cm), ending after patt Row 12 and a WS row. BO all 38 sts, pm at beg of this row.

MAIN SECTION

Neatly sew CO edge of lace border to BO edge to form a loop.

With RS facing and circ needle, beg and ending at m, pick up and knit 512 (536, 560, 584, 608, 632) sts evenly along one row-end edge of lace border. Join for working in rnds.

Rnd 1 (RS) Purl.

Rnd 2 *K1, k2tog, rep from * to last 2 sts, k2— 342 (358, 374, 390, 406, 422) sts.

Rnd 3 Purl.

Rnds 4 and 5 Knit.

Rnd 6 K0 (1, 1, 0, 1, 1), *yo, k2tog, k1, rep from * to last 0 (0, 1, 0, 0, 1) st, k0 (0, 1, 0, 0, 1).

Rnd 7 Knit.

Rnd 8 Purl.

Now work in rnds of St st (knit every rnd), as foll:

Work 0 (0, 4, 4, 8, 8) rnds.

Next rnd [K169 (177, 185, 193, 201, 209), k2tog, pm] twice— 340 (356, 372, 388, 404, 420) sts.

Work 8 rnds.

Next rnd [Knit to 2 sts before m, k2tog] twice.

Rep last 9 rnds 8 times more— 322 (338, 354, 370, 386, 402) sts.

Cont without further shaping until main section measures 10¼ (10½, 11, 11½, 12, 12¼)" (26 [26.5, 28, 29, 30.5, 31] cm), from pick-up rnd.

Now work yoke as foll:

Next rnd (dec rnd) *[K2tog] 5 (1, 0, 0, 0, 0) times, [k2, k2tog] 0 (0, 3, 7, 11, 15) times, [k1, k2tog] 47 (55, 51, 43, 35, 27) times, [k2tog, k2] 0 (0, 3, 7, 11, 15) times, [k2tog] 5 (1, 0, 0, 0, 0) times, rep from * once more— 208 (224, 240, 256, 272, 288) sts.

Next rnd K1, *p2, k2, rep from * to last 3 sts, p2, k1.

This rnd forms rib.

Work in rib until yoke measures 6" (15 cm) from dec rnd.

Next rnd (eyelet rnd) Rib 5, *yo, p2tog, rib 6, rep from * to last 3 sts, yo, p2tog, rib 1.

Work 10 more rnds in rib.

BO very loosely in rib.

HEM BORDER

CO 30 sts.

Row 1 K30.

Row 2 P25 and turn.

Row 3 K25.

Row 4 P25, k5.

Row 5 K5, p25.

Row 6 K25 and turn.

Row 7 P25.

Row 8 K30.

These 8 rows form patt.

Cont in patt until shorter row-end edge hem border measures 74 (76, 78, 80, 82, 85¾)" (188 [193, 198, 203, 208, 218] cm), ending after patt Row 8 and a WS row.

BO all 30 sts.

FINISHING

Neatly sew CO edge of hem border to BO

edge to form a loop. Lay free row-end edge of lace border over shorter edge of hem border so that upper 5 sts of hem border are covered, then neatly sew in place.

WAIST TIE

With U.S. size D-3 (3 mm) crochet hook make a length of ch approx 58 (60, 62, 64, 66, 68)" (147.5 [152.5, 157.5, 162.5, 167.5, 172.5] cm) long, turn and work 1 slip st into each ch to end.
Fasten off.
Thread tie through eyelet rnd as in photograph.

Cotton camisole

This design is based on a crisp white vintage camisole trimmed with lace. The original garments were worn as underwear (not seen in public) from the 19th century until Edwardian times, but my version is knitted in a pastel shade, turning it into a pretty summer top. It is knitted in 3-ply cotton, with a shaped yoke using simple lace stitches, with openwork front panels and shaping details on the back. A silk ribbon is threaded through the yoke for decoration. If you wish, you could further embellish the yoke with embroidery stitches, such as French knots, or cross stitches, like those used on the vest on page 51.

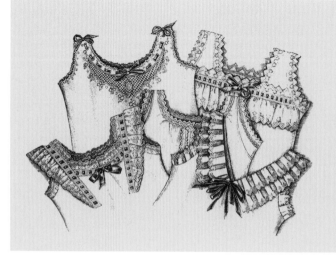

Camisole inspiration

In the late 19th century, pretty cotton camisoles with decorative lace and ribbon finishes were worn as underwear. My knitted version draws on their design.

FINISHED SIZE

To fit bust 32 (34, 36, 38, 40, 42)" (81.5 [86.5, 91.5, 96.5, 101.5, 106.5] cm).
Finished width (laid flat) 17½ (18¼, 19, 20¼, 21½, 22½)" (44.5 [46.5, 48.5, 51.5, 54.5, 57] cm).
Finished length (approx) 17½ (18, 18¾, 19¼, 20¼, 21¼)" (44.5 [45.5, 47.5, 50, 51.5, 54] cm).

YARN

Olympus "Emmy Grande Herbs" (100% cotton, 96 yd [88 m]/20 g), peach (171), 9 (9, 9, 10, 10, 11) balls.

NEEDLES

U.S. size 2 (2.75 mm) needles; U.S size 5 (3.75 mm) needles. Adjust needle size if necessary to obtain correct gauge.

NOTIONS

Stitch holder; 8 x 7/16" (11 mm) buttons; ¼" (7 mm) wide silk ribbon

GAUGE

36 stitches and 48 rows = 4" (10 cm) in stockinette stitch.

ABBREVIATIONS

See page 133.

BACK

Using U.S. size 2 (2.75 mm) needles, CO 157 (165, 171, 183, 193, 205) sts.
Beg with a RS row, work 2 rows in St st.
Next row (to form twisted hem) * K4, rotate left needle 360 degrees counterclockwise, rep from * to last 1 (1, 3, 3, 1, 1) st(s), k1 (1, 3, 3, 1, 1).
Cont as foll:
Row 1 (RS) P59 (63, 66, 72, 77, 83), [k1tbl, p1] 3 times, p8, [k1tbl, p1] 6 times, p8, [k1tbl, p1] 3 times, p58 (62, 65, 71, 76, 82).
Row 2 K59 (63, 66, 72, 77, 83), [p1tbl, k1] 3 times, k8, [p1tbl, k1] 6 times, k8 [p1tbl, k1] 3 times, k58 (62, 65, 71, 76, 82).
Rep Rows 1 and 2 4 (4, 4, 5, 5, 5) times more.
Next row (dec row) P2tog, p57 (61, 64, 70, 75, 81), [k1tbl, p1] twice, k1tbl, p2tog, p5, p2tog, [k1tbl, p1] 5 times, k1tbl, p2tog, p5, p2tog, [k1tbl, p1] 3 times, p56 (60, 63, 69, 74, 80), p2tog—151 (159, 165, 177, 187, 199) sts.
Next row K58 (62, 65, 71, 76, 82), [p1tbl, k1] 3

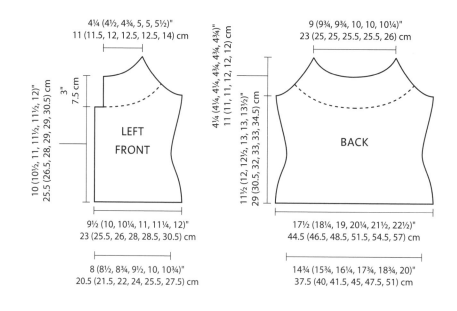

4¼ (4½, 4¾, 5, 5, 5½)"
11 (11.5, 12, 12.5, 12.5, 14) cm

9 (9¾, 9¾, 10, 10, 10¼)"
23 (25, 25, 25.5, 25.5, 26) cm

3"
7.5 cm

4¼ (4¼, 4¼, 4¾, 4¾, 4¾)"
11 (11, 11, 12, 12, 12) cm

10 (10½, 11, 11½, 11½, 12)"
25.5 (26.5, 28, 29, 29, 30.5) cm

11½ (12, 12½, 13, 13, 13½)"
29 (30.5, 32, 33, 33, 34.5) cm

LEFT FRONT

BACK

9½ (10, 10¼, 11, 11¼, 12)"
23 (25.5, 26, 28, 28.5, 30.5) cm

17½ (18¼, 19, 20¼, 21½, 22½)"
44.5 (46.5, 48.5, 51.5, 54.5, 57) cm

8 (8½, 8¾, 9½, 10, 10¾)"
20.5 (21.5, 22, 24, 25.5, 27.5) cm

14¾ (15¾, 16¼, 17¾, 18¾, 20)"
37.5 (40, 41.5, 45, 47.5, 51) cm

times, k6, [p1tbl, k1] 6 times, k6, [p1tbl, k1] 3 times, k57 (61, 64, 70, 75, 81).

Working in patt as set, dec in same place as set on foll 7th row, on foll 8th row, then on foll 6th row— 133 (141, 147, 159, 169, 181) sts.

Work 17 (17, 17, 19, 19, 19) rows even, ending with a WS row.

Next row (inc row) Inc in first st, k54 (58, 61, 67, 72, 78), [p1tbl, k1] twice, p1tbl, M1, k1, M1, [p1tbl, k1] 5 times, p1tbl, M1, k1, M1, [p1tbl, k1] 3 times, k53 (57, 60, 66, 71, 77), inc in last st— 139 (147, 153, 165, 175, 187) sts.

Inc as set every 10th row 3 times— 157 (165, 171, 183, 193, 205) sts.

Cont without shaping until Back measures 10 (10½, 11, 11½, 11½, 12)" (25.5 [26.5, 28, 29, 29, 30.5] cm), ending with a WS row.

Back Yoke
Right back
**Next row Work 69 (73, 76, 80, 85, 91) sts in patt, turn and leave rem sts on a stitch holder. Cont on these 69 (73, 76, 80, 85, 91) sts only.

Next row Patt to end.

Next row Patt 61 (63, 66, 72, 75, 79) sts, turn, and work to end of row.

Next row Patt 53 (54, 56, 64, 66, 68) sts, turn, and work to end of row.

Next row Patt 48 (49, 51, 59, 61, 63) sts, turn, and work to end of row.

Next row Patt 43 (44, 46, 54, 56, 58) sts, turn, and work to end of row.

Next row Patt 38 (39, 41, 49, 51, 53) sts, turn, and work to end of row.

Next row Patt 35 (36, 38, 45, 47, 49) sts, turn, and work to end of row.

Next row Patt 32 (33, 35, 41, 43, 46) sts, turn, and work to end of row.

Next row Patt 29 (30, 32, 38, 40, 43) sts, turn, and work to end of row.

Shape armhole
Next row (RS) BO 4 (5, 6, 6, 7, 7) sts, work 21 (22, 23, 29, 30, 32) sts (22 [23, 24, 30, 31, 33] sts on needle), turn, and work to end of row—65 (68, 70, 74, 78, 84) sts.

Next row BO 2 (3, 3, 3, 4, 5) sts, work 17 (17, 18, 24, 24, 25) sts, (18 [18, 19, 25, 25, 26] sts on needle), turn, and work to end of row—63 (65, 67, 71, 74, 79) sts.

Next row BO 2 (2, 3, 3, 3, 4) sts, work 13 (13, 13, 19, 19, 19) sts (14 [14, 14, 20, 20, 20] sts on needle), turn, and work to end of row—61 (63, 64, 68, 71, 75) sts.

Next row Dec 1 st, work 10 (10, 10, 16, 16, 16) sts (11 [11, 11, 17, 17, 17] sts on needle), turn, and work to end of row.

Next row Dec 1 st, work 7 (7, 7, 13, 13, 13) sts (8 [8, 8, 14, 14, 14] sts on needle), turn, and work to end of row.

Next row Dec 1 st, work 4 (4, 4, 10, 10, 10) sts (5 [5, 5, 11, 11, 11] sts on needle), turn, and work to end of row.

Next row Dec 1 st, work 1 (1, 1, 7, 7, 7) st(s) (2 [2, 2, 8, 8, 8] sts on needle), turn, and work to end of row— 57 (59, 60, 64, 67, 71) sts.

Sizes 38" (96.5 cm), 40" (101.5 cm), and 42" (106.5 cm) only
Next row Dec 1 st, work (4, 4, 4) sts ([5, 5, 5] sts on needle), turn, and work to end of row.

Next row Dec 1 st, work (1, 1, 1) st, ([2, 2, 2] sts on needle), turn, and work to end of row. ***
All sizes
Break yarn and leave rem 57 (59, 60, 62, 65, 69) sts on a holder.

Left Back
Working on sts left on a holder, keep center 19 (19, 19, 23, 23, 23) sts on holder, rejoin yarn, and work rem 69 (73, 76, 80, 85, 91) sts in same way as right yoke, reversing shapings and ending with a RS row.

Shape yoke

Next row (WS) Knit across 57 (59, 60, 62, 65, 69) sts left on needle, 19 (19, 19, 23, 23, 23) sts from stitch holder, and 57 (59, 60, 62, 65, 69) sts from right back—133 (137, 139, 147, 153, 161) sts.

Next row Knit to end and **AT SAME TIME** dec 2 sts across center sts—131 (135, 137, 145, 151, 159) sts.

Knit 3 rows even.

Next row Purl.

Cont as foll:

Row 1 K2 (1, 2, 1, 1, 1), *yo, k2tog, k1, rep from * to last 0 (2, 0, 0, 0, 2) sts, (yo, k2tog) 0 (1, 0, 0, 0, 1) time.

Row 2 Purl.

Rows 3 and 4 Knit.

Row 5 (dec row) K11 (6, 3, 4, 7, 5), * k2tog, k10 (15, 12, 10, 10, 9) rep from * to last 0 (10, 8, 9, 0, 11) sts, k2tog [0 (1, 1, 1, 0, 1)] time, ko (8, 6, 7, 0, 9)—121 (127, 127, 133, 139, 145) sts.

Row 6 Knit.

Row 7 K1, * k2tog, yo, k1, yo, skp, k1, rep from * to end.

Row 8 P2tog, * yo, p3, yo, p3tog, rep from * to last 5 sts, yo, p3, yo, p2tog.

Row 9 K1, * yo, skp, k1, k2tog, yo, k1, rep from * to end.

Row 10 * P2, yo, p3tog, yo, p1, rep from * to last st, p1.

Rows 11 and 12 Knit.

Row 13 (dec row) K11 (6, 3, 4, 5, 5), * k2tog, k9 (14, 11, 9, 8, 8) rep from * to last 0 (9, 7, 8, 0, 10) sts, k2tog [0 (1, 1, 1, 1, 0)] time, ko (7, 5, 6, 0, 8)—111 (119, 117, 121, 127, 131) sts.

Rows 14 and 15 Knit.

Row 16 Purl.

Rows 17 and 18 Knit.

Row 19 K1, * yo, k2tog, rep from * to last 2 sts, k2.

Row 20 Knit.

Row 21 (dec row) K11 (9, 7, 4, 7, 5), * k2tog, k8 (9, 9, 8, 8, 7) rep from * to last 0 (0, 0, 7, 0, 9) sts, k2tog [0 (0, 0, 1, 0, 1)] time, ko (0, 0, 5, 0, 7)—101 (109, 107, 109, 115, 117) sts.

Rows 22 and 23 Knit.

Row 24 K3 (3, 1, 3, 1, 3), * (k1, p1, k1) all in next st, p3tog, rep from * last 2 sts, k2.

Row 25 Purl.

Row 26 K3 (3, 1, 3, 1, 3), * p3tog, [k1, p1, k1] all in next st, rep from * to last 2 sts, k2.

Row 27 Purl.

Row 28 Knit.

Row 29 (dec row) K11 (8, 3, 4, 7, 5), * k2tog, k7 (11, 9, 7, 7, 6) rep from * to last 0 (10, 5, 6, 9, 8) sts, k2tog [0 (1, 1, 1, 1, 1)] time, ko (8, 3, 4, 7, 6)—91 (101, 97, 97, 103, 103) sts.

Rows 30 and 31 Knit.

Row 32 Purl.

Row 33 Knit.

Row 34 Purl.

Row 35 and 36 Knit.

Row 37 (dec row) K8 (4, 7, 8, 7, 3), * k2tog, k6 (5, 7, 14, 6, 8) rep from * to last 3 (6, 0, 9, 8, 0) sts, k2tog [0 (1, 0, 1, 1, 0)] time, k3 (4, 0, 7, 6, 0)—81 (87, 87, 91, 91, 93) sts.

Row 38 Purl.

Row 39 K2 * yo, k2tog, k1, rep from * to last 1 (1, 1, 2, 2, 1) st(s), k1 (1, 1, 2, 2, 1).

Row 40 Purl.

Rows 41 and 42 Knit.

BO using U.S. size 5 (3.75 mm) needles.

LEFT FRONT

Bead St (panel of 7 sts)

Row 1 K1, k2tog, yo, k1, yo, skp, k1.

Row 2 P2tog, yo, p3, yo, p2tog.

Row 3 K1, yo, skp, k1, k2tog, yo, k1.

Row 4 P2, yo, p3tog, yo, p2.

Using U.S. size 2 (2.75 mm) needles, CO 85 (89, 92, 98, 102, 109) sts.

Beg with a RS row, work 2 rows in St st.

Next row (to form twisted hem) * K4, rotate left

needle 360 degrees counterclockwise, rep from * to last 1 (1, 4, 2, 2, 1) st(s), k1 (1, 4, 2, 2, 1).

Cont as foll:

Next row (RS) P44 (48, 51, 57, 61, 68), k2, yo, skp, p3, work 7 sts as set on Row 1 of Bead St, [p1, k1tbl] 3 times, p1, k2, yo, skp, p7, k9.

Next row P9, k9, yo, k2tog, [k1, p1tbl] 3 times, k1, work 7 sts as set on Row 2 of Bead St, k5, yo, k2tog, k44 (48, 51, 57, 61, 68).

These 2 rows set patt placement.

Work 7 (7, 7, 9, 9, 9) rows more, ending with a RS row.

Next row (dec row) P9, k9, yo, k2tog, [k1, p1tbl] 3 times, k1, work 7 sts in Bead St, k5, yo, k2tog, k5, skp, k2tog, k33 (37, 40, 46, 50, 57), k2tog—82 (86, 89, 95, 99, 106) sts.

Work 7 rows even in patt.

Next row (dec row) P9, k9, yo, k2tog, [k1, p1tbl] 3 times, k1, work 7 sts in Bead St, k5, yo, k2tog, k4, skp, k2tog, k31 (35, 38, 44, 48, 55), k2tog—79 (83, 86, 92, 96, 103) sts.

Cont to dec as set in same place every 8th row twice more, then dec 1 st at end only of foll 6th row—72 (76, 79, 85, 89, 96) sts.

Work 16 (16, 16, 18, 18, 18) rows without shaping, ending with a RS row.

Next row (inc row) P9, k9, yo, k2tog, [k1, p1tbl] 3 times, k1, work 7 sts in Bead St, k5, yo, k2tog, k2, M1, k2, M1, k26 (30, 33, 39, 43, 50), inc in last st—75 (79, 82, 88, 92, 99) sts.

Work 9 rows even in patt.

Next row (inc row) P9, k9, yo, k2tog, [k1, p1tbl] 3 times, k1, work 7 sts in Bead St, k5, yo, k2tog, k3, M1, k2, M1, k28 (32, 35, 41, 45, 52), inc in last st—78 (82, 85, 91, 95, 102) sts.

Cont to inc as set every 10th row twice more— 84 (88, 91, 97, 101, 108) sts.

Cont in patt without shaping until work matches Back to beg of yoke, ending with a WS row.

Left Front Yoke

Next row (RS) Patt 69 (73, 76, 80, 85, 91) sts and turn, leave rem 15 (15, 15, 17, 16, 17) sts on holder.

Cont on these 69 (73, 76, 80, 85, 91) sts only. Work as for Right Back from ** to ***, keeping front panel pattern correct.

Next row (RS) Patt across all sts, then work across sts left on holder as foll: P5 (5, 6, 7, 6, 7), k9—72 (74, 75, 79, 81, 86) sts.

Next row BO 5 (5, 5, 6, 6, 7) sts, knit to end—67 (69, 70, 73, 75, 79) sts.

Knit 3 rows even.

Next row Purl.

Cont as foll:

Row 1 K1 (2, 1, 1, 2, 1), * yo, k2tog, k1, rep from * to last 0 (1, 0, 0, 1, 0) st, k0 (1, 0, 0, 1, 0).

Row 2 Purl.

Rows 3 and 4 Knit.

Row 5 (dec row) K5 (6, 17, 6, 5, 6), * k2tog, k9 (6, 15, 10, 7, 11), rep from * to last 7 (7, 19, 7, 7, 8) sts, k2tog, k5 (5, 17, 5, 5, 6)—61 (61, 67, 67, 67, 73) sts.

Row 6 Knit.

Row 7 K1, * k2tog, yo, k1, yo, skp, k1, rep from * to end.

Row 8 P2tog, * yo, p3, yo, p3tog, rep from * to last 5 sts, yo, p3, yo, p2tog.

Row 9 K1, * yo, skp, k1, k2tog, yo, k1, rep from * to end.

Row 10 * P2, yo, p3tog, yo, p1, rep from * to last st, p1.

Rows 11 and 12 Knit.

Row 13 (dec row) K6 (6, 17, 5, 6, 6), * k2tog, k10 (6, 14, 12, 7, 13) rep from * to last 7 (7, 18, 6, 7, 7) sts, k2tog, k5 (5, 16, 4, 5, 5)—56 (54, 64, 62, 60, 68) sts.

Row 14 Knit.

Row 15 Knit to end and **AT SAME TIME** dec 3 (1, 3, 1, 1, 3) sts evenly across row—53 (53, 61, 61, 59, 65) sts.

Row 16 Purl.

Rows 17 and 18 Knit.

Row 19 K1, * yo, k2tog, rep from * to last 2 st, k2.

Row 20 Knit.

Row 21 (dec row) K6 (17, 7, 6, 18, 7), k2tog, k11* (15, 7, 14, 19, 14), k2tog, rep to last 6 (17, 7, 5, 18, 8) sts, k6 (17, 7, 5, 18, 8)—49 (51, 55, 57, 57, 61) sts.

Rows 22 and 23 Knit.

Row 24 K3 (1, 1, 3, 3, 3), * [k1, p1, k1] all in next st, p3tog, rep from * last 2 sts, k2.

Row 25 Purl.

Row 26 K3 (1, 1, 3, 3, 3), * p3tog, [k1, p1, k1] all in next st, rep from * to last 2 sts, k2.

Row 27 Purl.

Row 28 Knit.

Row 29 (dec row) Knit to end and **AT SAME TIME** dec 6 sts evenly across row—43 (45, 49, 51, 51, 55) sts.

Rows 30 and 31 Knit.

Row 32 Purl.

Row 33 Knit.

Row 34 Purl.

Row 35 and 36 Knit.

Row 37 (dec row) Knit to end and **AT SAME TIME** dec 4 (4, 6, 6, 6, 6) sts evenly across row—39 (41, 43, 45, 45, 49) sts.

Row 38 Purl.

Row 39 K2 (2, 1, 2, 2, 1)* yo, k2tog, k1, rep from * to last 1 (0, 0, 1, 1, 0) st, k1 (0, 0, 1, 1, 0).

Row 40 Purl.

Rows 41 and 42 Knit.

BO using U.S. size 5 (3.75 mm) needles.

Place markers for buttons along front edge, first to fall approx 1¼" (3 cm) from BO edge, last to fall ½" (1.3 cm) down from BO at front neck and rem 6 spread evenly between.

RIGHT FRONT

Using U.S. size 2 (2.75 mm) needles, CO 85 (89,

92, 98, 102, 109) sts.

Beg with a RS row, work 2 rows in St st.

Next row (to form twisted hem) * K4, rotate left needle 360 degrees counterclockwise, rep from * to last 1 (1, 4, 2, 2, 1) st(s), k1 (1, 4, 2, 2, 1). Cont as foll:

Next row (RS) K9, p7, k2, yo, skp, [p1, k1tbl] 3 times, p1, work 7 sts as set on Row 1 of Bead St, p3, k2, yo, skp, p44 (48, 51, 57, 61, 68).

Next row K46 (50, 53, 59, 63, 70), yo, k2tog, [k1, p1tbl] 3 times, k1, work 7 sts as set on Row 2 of Bead St, k5, yo, k2tog, k7, p9.

These 2 rows set patt placement.

Complete as given for Left Front, reversing all shapings and adding 8 evenly spaced buttonholes to match markers on left front at beg of RS rows as foll:

Buttonhole row K4, BO 2 sts, patt to end.

Next row Work to buttonhole, CO 2 sts, p4.

STRAPS (Make 2)

Using U.S. size 2 (2.75 mm) needles, CO 32 (32, 38, 38, 44, 44) sts.

Knit 2 rows.

Next row Purl.

Next row K2, *yo, k2tog, k1, rep from * to end.

Next row Purl.

Knit 2 rows.

BO using U.S. size 5 (3.75 mm) needles.

You should now be able to check the length of your armhole by basting this strap in position to front and back and trying your garment for size. If you wish to alter the length of strap you will need to add or detract in multiples of 3 to make the pattern work.

Sew each strap to Fronts and Back, so it matches with pattern of yoke.

LACE EDGING

Using U.S. size 2 (2.75 mm) needles, CO 4 sts.

Rows 1, 3, and 6 Knit.

Row 2 K2, yo, k2—5 sts.

Row 4 K3, yo, k2—6 sts.

Row 5 K2, yo, k2tog, yo, k2—7 sts.

Row 7 K3, yo, k2tog, yo, k2—8 sts.

Row 8 BO 4 sts, K to end—4 sts.

These 8 rows form patt. Cont in patt until lace edging fits around entire neck edge without stretching and sewing in position at same time.

Work armhole edgings in same way.

FINISHING

Join side seams.

RIGHT FRONT EDGING

With RS tog, using U.S. size 2 (2.75 mm) needles, pick up and knit 84 (86, 86, 92, 95, 99) sts evenly along front edge from CO edge to top of button band.

Knit 2 rows.

BO using U.S. size 5 (3.75 mm) needles.

Work Left Front edging to match.

Sew on buttons and thread ribbon through top eyelets around neck.

How to embroider knots and flowers

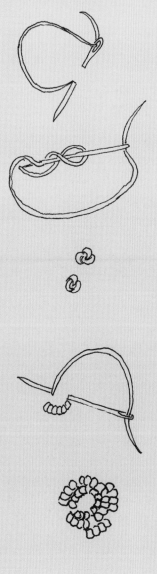

You could add a row of French knots and little embroidered flowers with bullion knots to the yoke as decoration if you wish. Alternatively, use a row of cross stitches (see page 55).

To make knots

1 Thread needle with chosen yarn, insert into WS of work and bring needle through to front and start to make a tiny stitch.

2 Twist the yarn around the needle two or three times and then push the needle back through work close to point of entry, holding the yarn twists with your finger so that they form a tiny ball on the front of the work. Continue to make small French knots as required.

To make flowers

1 Follow step 1 above, then wrap the yarn around the needle six or seven times. Then insert the needle back into the work a little distance from the entry point, pushing the yarn wraps off the needle to make a long coil.

2 Repeat to form enough scattered semicircles to form a flower.

Heart lavender bags

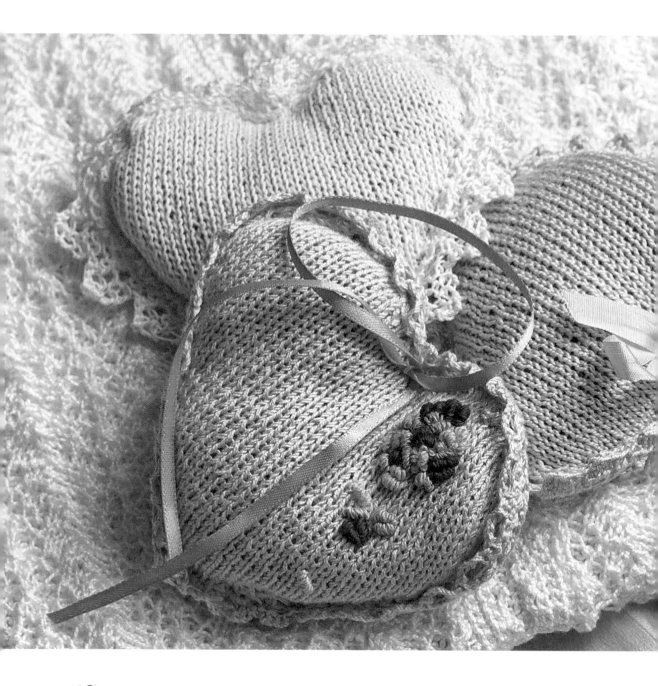

If you have some yarn leftover, you could turn it to good use by making some pretty little lavender bags. They make charming gifts, stuffed with dried lavender. Pretty them up with a simple lacy edging and a few embroidery stitches, such as French knots or cross stitches. You could also decorate them with a few bugle beads, too, if you have some leftover from one of the beaded projects.

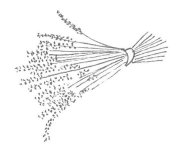

Lavender bag inspiration

This small embroidered pillow from a home-crafts book of the early 20th century—when making and embroidering objects for the home was widespread—inspired my lavender bags.

FINISHED SIZE

Size will vary according to yarn used.

YARN

Any yarn can be used but these were made using size 20 crochet cotton—you will need approx 5 g.

NEEDLES AND CROCHET HOOK

Straight needles in size appropriate to yarn being used, and another pair one size finer for knitted edging; for crochet edging, appropriate size crochet hook.

NOTIONS

Lavender or pot pourri to fill bags; stitch holder.

GAUGE

This is not important as finished size can vary.

ABBREVIATIONS

See page 133.
Crochet instructions use U.S. terms, see page 133 for U.K. equivalents.

NOTES

These lavender bags were made using size 20 crochet cotton and needles sizes given here are sizes used for this yarn. Vary needle size to match your chosen yarn.

Instructions are given for three different edgings—two knitted and one crocheted. Make whichever you prefer.

FRONT AND BACK (Both alike)

With U.S. size 1 (2.25 mm) needles, CO 3 sts.
Beg with a RS row, work in St st throughout as foll:
Work 2 rows.
Inc 1 st at each end of next 9 rows, then on every other row 10 times—41 sts.
Work 9 rows, ending with a WS row.

Shape top

Row 1 (RS) K1, skp, k17, and turn, leaving rem 21 sts on st holder.
Work on this set of sts only for first side of top.
Row 2 Purl to last 3 sts, p2tog tbl, p1—18 sts.
**Row 3 K1, skp, knit to last 3 sts, k2tog, k1—16 sts.
Row 4 P1, p2tog, purl to last 3 sts, p2tog tbl, p1—14 sts.
Rows 5 and 6 As Rows 3 and 4.
BO rem 10 sts.**
With RS tog, rejoin yarn to 21 sts on holder, k2tog, knit to last 3 sts, k2tog, k1—19 sts.
Row 2 P1, p2tog, purl to end—18 sts.
Complete as given for first side from ** to **.

FIRST KNITTED LACE EDGING

Using U.S. size 0 (2 mm) needles, CO 4 sts.
Row 1 Knit.
Row 2 K2, yo, k2—5 sts.
Row 3 Knit.
Row 4 K3, yo, k2—6 sts.
Row 5 K2, yo, k2tog, yo, k2—7 sts.
Row 6 Knit.
Row 7 K3, yo, k2tog, yo, k2—8 sts.
Row 8 BO 4 sts, knit to end—4 sts.
Rep these 8 rows until edging fits neatly around entire outer edge of one knitted piece, ending with a Row 8.
BO rem 4 sts.

SECOND KNITTED LACE EDGING

Using U.S. size 0 (2 mm) needles, CO 6 sts.
Row 1 Sl 1, k2, yo, k3—7 sts.
Row 2 K6, p1.
Row 3 Sl 1, k2, yo, k1, yo, k3—9 sts.
Row 4 BO 3 sts purlwise, purl to last st, k1—6 sts.

Rep these 4 rows until edging fits neatly around entire outer edge of one knitted piece, ending with a Row 4.
BO rem 6 sts.

FINISHING

Join CO and BO ends of edging. Sew front and back pieces together, sandwiching straight edge of edging in seam and remembering to insert filling before closing seam.

CROCHET EDGING

With U.S. size 1 steel (2 mm) crochet hook, holding front and back WS together and working through edges of both knitted pieces to join them together, and remembering to insert filling before completing rnd, work 94 sc evenly around entire outer edge of knitted pieces, ending with slip st to first sc.

Next rnd Ch 1 (does NOT count as st), 1 sc into each sc to end, working 3 sc into base corner point and ending with slip st to first sc—96 sts.

Next rnd Ch 1 (does NOT count as st), 1 sc into first sc, *4 ch, skip 1 sc, 1 sc into each of next 2 sc, rep from * to end, replacing sc at end of last rep with slip st to first sc.
Fasten off.

Wrapover cardigan

Inspired by the 18th-century short jacket, known as a spencer, which often had extra-long sleeves. I've made these sleeves long, although they could be worn with the rib turned back. I've also made the ties extra long to form a bow at the front, but these could be made shorter or left off completely and the cardigan fastened with a brooch.

Wrapover cardigan inspiration

The inspiration for this cropped cardigan comes from the short spencer jackets of the 18th century, worn over Empire-line dresses as seen illustrated here.

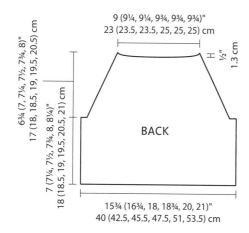

9 (9¼, 9¼, 9¾, 9¾, 9¾)"
23 (23.5, 23.5, 25, 25, 25) cm

½"
1.3 cm

6¾ (7, 7¼, 7½, 19, 19.5, 20.5, 8)"
17 (18, 18.5, 19, 19.5, 20.5, 21) cm

BACK

7 (7¼, 7½, 19, 19.5, 20.5, 8¼)"
18 (18.5, 19, 19.5, 20.5, 21) cm

15¾ (16¾, 18, 18¾, 20, 21)"
40 (42.5, 45.5, 47.5, 51, 53.5) cm

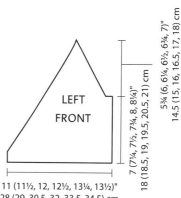

5¾ (6, 6¼, 6½, 6¾, 7)"
14.5 (15, 16, 16.5, 17, 18) cm

LEFT FRONT

7 (7¼, 7½, 19, 19.5, 20.5, 8¼)"
18 (18.5, 19, 19.5, 20.5, 21) cm

11 (11½, 12, 12½, 13¼, 13½)"
28 (29, 30.5, 32, 33.5, 34.5) cm

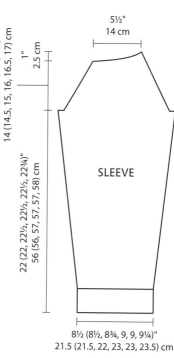

5½"
14 cm

1"
2.5 cm

5½ (5¾, 6, 6¼, 6½, 6¾)"
14 (14.5, 15, 16, 16.5, 17) cm

SLEEVE

22 (22, 22½, 22½, 22½, 22¾)"
56 (56, 57, 57, 57, 58) cm

8½ (8½, 8¾, 9, 9, 9¼)"
21.5 (21.5, 22, 23, 23, 23.5) cm

13¼ (13½, 13¾, 14, 14¼, 14¾)"
33.5 (34.5, 35, 35.5, 36, 37.5) cm

FINISHED SIZE

To fit bust 32 (34, 36, 38, 40, 42)" (81.5 [86.5, 91.5, 96.5, 101.5, 106.5] cm).

Actual bust measurement 31½ (33½, 36, 37½, 40, 42)" (80 [85, 91.5, 95, 101.5, 106.5] cm).

Finished length 13¾ (14¼, 14¾, 15¼, 15¾, 16¼)" (35 [36, 37.5, 38.5, 40, 41.5] cm).

Sleeve length 22 (22, 22½, 22½, 22½, 22¾)" (56 [56, 57, 57, 57, 58] cm).

YARN

Lace-weight yarn:

Rowan "Fine Lace" (80% baby suri alpaca, 20% extra fine merino, 437 yd [400 m]/50 g): pink (Antique 921), 5 (5, 6, 6, 7, 7) balls.

NEEDLES

U.S. size 2/3 (3 mm) needles: one pair straight needles and one circular (circ) needle; U.S. size 3 (3.25 mm) needles. Adjust needle size if necessary to obtain correct gauge.

NOTIONS

Stitch holders.

GAUGE

With yarn **DOUBLE**, 27 stitches and 37 rows = 4" (10 cm) in stockinette stitch.

ABBREVIATIONS

See page 133.

BACK

Using U.S. size 2/3 (3 mm) needles and yarn **DOUBLE**, CO 107 (113, 121, 127, 135, 141) sts.

Row 1 (RS) K1, *p1, k1, rep from * to end.

Row 2 P1, *k1, p1, rep from * to end.

These 2 rows form rib.

Work in rib for 13 more rows, ending with a RS row.

Row 16 (WS) Rib 3 (6, 6, 4, 4, 7), inc in next st, [rib 10 (10, 11, 12, 13, 13), inc in next st] 9 times, rib 4 (7, 6, 5, 4, 7)— 117 (123, 131, 137, 145, 151) sts.

Change to U.S. size 3 (3.25 mm) needles.

Beg with a RS row, now work in St st throughout as foll:

Work 52 (54, 56, 58, 60, 62) rows, ending with a WS row.

Shape raglan armholes

BO 5 sts at beg of next 2 rows, then 2 sts at beg of foll 2 rows— 103 (109, 117, 123, 131, 137) sts.

Sizes 40" (101.5 cm) and 42" (106.5 cm) only

Next row (RS) K3, k2tog, knit to last 5 sts, skp, k3— 2 sts dec'd.

Next row P3, p2tog tbl, purl to last 5 sts, p2tog, p3— 2 sts dec'd.

Rep last 2 rows (1, 3) time(s) more—(123, 121) sts.

All sizes

Next row (RS) K3, k2tog, knit to last 5 sts, skp, k3— 2 sts dec'd.

Working all raglan armhole decreases as set by last row, dec 1 st at each end of every 4th (4th, 4th, 4th, 2nd, 2nd) row once, every 4th row 5 (4, 1, 0, 0, 0) time(s), then every other row 14 (17, 24, 27, 27, 26) times— 61 (63, 63, 65, 65, 65) sts.

Work 1 row, ending with a WS row.

Shape back neck

Next row (RS) K3, k2tog, k2 and turn, leaving rem sts on a st holder.

Work on this set of 6 sts only for first side of neck.

Next row P2tog, p4— 5 sts.

Next row K2, sk2p— 3 sts.

Next row P2tog, p1— 2 sts.

Next row K2tog and fasten off rem st.

With RS tog, slip center 47 (49, 49, 51, 51, 51) sts onto another st holder, rejoin yarn to rem sts, k2, skp, k3— 6 sts.

Next row P4, p2tog— 5 sts.

Next row K3tog, k2— 3 sts.

Next row P1, p2tog— 2 sts.

Next row K2tog and fasten off rem st.

LEFT FRONT

Using U.S. size 2/3 (3 mm) needles and yarn **DOUBLE**, CO 75 (77, 81, 85, 89, 91) sts.

Work in rib as given for back for 15 rows, ending with a RS row.

Row 16 (WS) Rib 7 (5, 5, 8, 8, 8), inc in next st, [rib 14 (12, 13, 16, 17, 14), inc in next st] 4 (5, 5, 4, 4, 5) times, rib 7 (6, 5, 8, 8, 7)— 80 (83, 87, 90, 94, 97) sts.

Change to U.S. size 3 (3.25 mm) needles.

Beg with a RS row, now work in St st throughout as foll:

Work 2 rows, ending with a WS row.

Shape front slope

Sizes 32" (81.5 cm) and 34" (86.5 cm) only

Next row (RS) Knit to last 4 sts, skp, k2— 1 st dec'd.

Next row P2, p2tog tbl, purl to end— 1 st dec'd.

Rep last 2 rows 1 (0) time(s) more— 76 (81) sts.

All sizes

Next row (RS) Knit to last 4 sts, skp, k2— 1 st dec'd.

Working all front slope decreases as set by last

row, dec 1 st at front slope edge of every 2nd (2nd, 4th, 4th, 4th) row once, every 4th row 0 (0, 0, 1, 3, 5) time(s), then every other row 21 (23, 24, 23, 20, 17) times—53 (56, 61, 64, 69, 73) sts.

Work 1 row, ending with a WS row.

Shape raglan armhole

BO at beg of RS rows 5 sts once, then 2 sts once and **AT SAME TIME** dec 1 st at front slope edge every other row—44 (47, 52, 55, 60, 64) sts.

Work 1 row.

Dec 1 st at raglan armhole edge of every row 1 (1, 1, 1, 5, 9) time(s), every 4th row 6 (5, 2, 1, 0, 0) time(s), then every other row 8 (11, 18, 21, 22, 21) times and **AT SAME TIME**, dec 1 st at front slope edge of next row, then every other row 20 (21, 22, 23, 24, 25) times—8 sts.

Work 1 row, ending with a WS row.

Next row (RS) K3, k3tog, k2—6 sts.

Next row Purl.

Next row K3, k3tog—4 sts.

Next row Purl.

Next row K1, sk2p—2 sts.

Next row Purl.

Next row K2tog and fasten off rem st.

RIGHT FRONT

Using U.S. size 2/3 (3 mm) needles and yarn **DOUBLE**, CO 75 (77, 81, 85, 89, 91) sts.

Work in rib as given for back for 15 rows, ending with a RS row.

Next row (WS) Rib 7 (6, 5, 8, 8, 7), inc in next st, [rib 14 (12, 13, 16, 17, 14), inc in next st] 4 (5, 5, 4, 4, 5) times, rib 7 (5, 5, 8, 8, 8)—80 (83, 87, 90, 94, 97) sts.

Change to U.S. size 3 (3.25 mm) needles.

Beg with a RS row, now work in St st throughout as foll:

Work 2 rows, ending with a WS row.

Shape front slope

Size 32" (81.5 cm) and 34" (86.5 cm) only

Next row (RS) K2, k2tog, knit to end—1 st dec'd.

Next row Purl to last 4 sts, p2tog, p2—1 st dec'd.

Rep last 2 rows 1 (0) time(s) more—76 (81) sts.

All sizes

Next row (RS) K2, k2tog, knit to end—1 st dec'd.

Working all front slope decreases as set by last row, dec 1 st at front slope edge of 2nd (2nd, 4th, 4th, 4th) row once, every 4th row 0 (0, 0, 1, 3, 5) time(s), then every other row 21 (23, 24, 23, 20, 17) times—53 (56, 61, 64, 69, 73) sts.

Work 1 row, ending with a WS row.

Shape raglan armhole

Dec 1 st at front slope edge of next then every other row once and **AT SAME TIME** BO at beg of WS rows 5 sts once, then 2 sts once—44 (47, 52, 55, 60, 64) sts.

Dec 1 st at raglan armhole edge of every row 1 (1, 1, 1, 5, 9) time(s), every 4th row 6 (5, 2, 1, 0, 0) time(s), then every other row 8 (11, 18, 21, 22, 21) times, and **AT SAME TIME**, dec 1 st at front slope edge of next row, then every other row 20 (21, 22, 23, 24, 25) times—8 sts.

Work 1 row, ending with a WS row.

Next row (RS) K2, sk2p, k3—6 sts.

Next row Purl.

Next row Sk2p, k3—4 sts.

Next row Purl.

Next row K3tog, k1—2 sts.

Next row Purl.

Next row K2tog and fasten off rem st.

SLEEVES

With U.S. size 2/3 (3 mm) needles and yarn **DOUBLE**, CO 57 (57, 59, 61, 61, 63) sts.

Work in rib as given for back for 30 rows,

ending with a WS row.

Change to U.S. size 3 (3.25 mm) needles.

Beg with a RS row, now work in St st, shaping sides by inc 1 st at each end of 9th row, every 8th row 0 (0, 0, 0, 2, 0) times, every 10th row 10 (17, 17, 17, 16, 18) times, then every 12th row 6 (0, 0, 0, 0, 0) times—89 (91, 93, 95, 97, 99) sts. Cont without further shaping until sleeve measures 22 (22, 22½, 22½, 22½, 22¾)" (56 [56, 57, 57, 57, 58] cm), ending with a WS row.

Shape raglan

BO 5 sts at beg of next 2 rows, then 2 sts at beg of foll 2 rows—75 (77, 79, 81, 83, 85) sts. Working all raglan decreases in same way as back raglan armhole decreases, dec 1 st at each end of next row, every 4th row 5 times, then every other row 13 (14, 15, 16, 17, 18) times—37 sts.

Work 1 row, ending with a WS row.

Left sleeve only

Row 1 (RS) K3, k2tog, knit to last 7 sts, wrap next st (by slipping next st from left needle to right needle, taking yarn to opposite side of work between needles, and then slipping same st back onto left needle) and turn.

Row 2 Purl.

Row 3 K3, k2tog, k19, wrap next st, and turn.

Row 4 Purl.

Row 5 K3, k2tog, k13, wrap next st, and turn.

Row 6 Purl.

Row 7 K3, k2tog, k7, wrap next st, and turn.

Row 8 Purl.

Row 9 K3, k2tog, k1, wrap next st, and turn.

Row 10 Purl.

Break yarn and leave all 32 sts on a st holder.

Right sleeve only

Row 1 (RS) K3, k2tog, knit to last 5 sts, skp, k3.

Row 2 P29, wrap next st, and turn.

Row 3 Knit to last 5 sts, skp, k3.

Row 4 P23, wrap next st, and turn.

Row 5 Knit to last 5 sts, skp, k3.

Row 6 P17, wrap next st, and turn.

Row 7 Knit to last 5 sts, skp, k3.

Row 8 P11, wrap next st, and turn.

Row 9 Knit to last 5 sts, skp, k3.

Row 10 P5, wrap next st, and turn.

Break yarn and leave all 32 sts on a st holder.

FRONT BAND AND TIES

Join all raglan seams.

With RS tog, U.S. size 2/3 (3 mm) circular needle and yarn **DOUBLE**, starting and ending at front CO edges, pick up and knit 80 (84, 88, 92, 96, 100) sts up right front opening edge to front raglan seam, work across 32 sts on right sleeve holder as foll: K2, [skp, k3] 6 times, pick up and knit 2 sts down right back neck, work across 47 (49, 49, 51, 51, 51) sts on back holder as foll: K2 (3, 3, 4, 4, 4), [k2tog, k4] 7 times, k2tog, k1 (2, 2, 3, 3, 3), pick up and knit 2 sts up left back neck, work across 32 sts on left sleeve holder as foll: [k3, k2tog] 6 times, k2, then pick up and knit 80 (84, 88, 92, 96, 100) sts down left front opening edge—255 (265, 273, 283, 291, 299) sts.

Starting with Row 2, work in rib as given for back for 5 rows, ending with a WS row.

Next row (RS) Rib 12 and slip these sts onto a holder (for right tie), BO next 231 (241, 249, 259, 267, 275) sts, rib to end.

Work on this last set of 12 sts only for left tie.

Work in rib until tie measures 34 (35, 36, 37, 38, 39)" (86.5 [89, 91.5, 94, 96.5, 99] cm), ending with a WS row.

BO.

Rejoin yarn to 12 sts on right tie holder and work to match left tie.

FINISHING

Sew side and sleeve seams, leaving a small opening in right side seam for tie to pass through.

Crochet necklace and bracelet

If you have some broken necklaces, or a collection of vintage beads, you can reuse them to create some lovely new jewelry with the simplest crochet chain stitch and fine crochet cotton. You could wear the necklace long, 1920s style, or wrap it around twice. The bracelet is made using the same principle but with clusters of seed beads together wtih the larger beads. For a chunkier version, opt for bigger beads and perhaps crochet with a matching fine ribbon yarn rather than fine cotton.

Jewelry inspiration

Until the 1960s jewelry sets were popular—as can be seen in this illustration from the 50s—necklace, bracelet, earrings, and brooch all go together. The beauty of making your own jewelry, like the necklace and bracelet here, lies in being able to match the pieces.

FINISHED SIZE

Size will vary according to yarn and number of beads used. This necklace is approx 40" (101.5 cm) long and the bracelet is approx 15" (38 cm) long.

YARN

Any yarn can be used. This necklace was made using size 20 crochet cotton, and the bracelet was made with size 5 crochet cotton.

CROCHET HOOKS

Appropriate size crochet hook for yarn being used. This necklace was made using U.S. size 1 steel (2 mm) crochet hook, and the bracelet with U.S. size C-2 (2.75 mm) crochet hook.

NOTIONS

Selection of faceted glass and seed beads— either new or old vintage from a broken necklace, as here. This necklace used 88 beads and the bracelet used 75 beads.

GAUGE

This is not important as finished size can vary.

ABBREVIATIONS

See page 133.
Crochet instructions use U.S. terms, see page 133 for U.K. equivalents.

NECKLACE

Thread beads onto yarn, alternating one faceted and one seed bead along length. Using U.S. size 1 steel (2 mm) crochet hook, make ch 4, *slide a bead up next to hook and work ch 1 behind bead, ch 4, rep from * until either necklace is required length or all beads are used up, and replacing "ch 4" at end of last rep with "slip st into first ch."
Fasten off.

BRACELET

Thread beads onto yarn, alternating types of beads and grouping 2, 3, or 4 seed beads together.
Using U.S. size C-2 (2.75 mm) crochet hook, ch 3, *slide a bead (or group of seed beads) up next to hook and work ch 1 behind bead(s), ch 3, rep from * until all beads are used up, turn.
Next row Ch 1 (does NOT count as st), 1 sc into each ch to end.
Fasten off.

Working with beads

Firstly, you need to thread the beads you plan to use onto the working yarn. You can break the yarn at the point at which you add the beads. Make sure the hole of the beads chosen is large enough to allow the eye of a sewing needle to pass through it.

1 Thread the needle with a short length of sewing thread, and knot the ends together to make a loop.

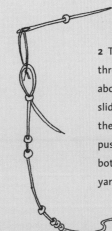

2 Thread your yarn through the loop for about 3" (7.5 cm). Then slide the beads onto the sewing needle and push them down over both loops onto the yarn.

3 Move the beads up the yarn when you are ready to crochet with them.

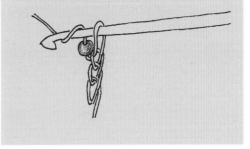

Lace-edged camisole

Garter stitch always seems to me to have a lovely "old-fashioned" look, but it also takes longer to knit than stockinette stitch—particularly in a fine yarn! So I designed this very simple camisole, which could be worn as an undergarment—perhaps knitted in silk or a fine cashmere—or is pretty enough to be seen and worn as a top. I've chosen to knit the body in 3-ply wool and the lace border in a crochet cotton, but the whole garment could be made in one yarn. It is finished with a lace edging around the neck and armholes, sewn together to form the straps. I've added a touch of color with simple cross-stitch embroidery in red cotton—giving it an authentic vintage look.

Lace edge inspiration

Knitted woolen underwear continued to be worn up until the 1960s. Women's magazines often featured knitting patterns for underwear for adults and children. This vest, taken from a magazine of the 1940s, with its pretty lace edging and ribbed waist, inspired my version.

FINISHED SIZE

To fit bust 32 (34, 36, 38, 40, 42)" (81.5 [86.5, 91.5, 96.5, 101.5, 106.5] cm).

Actual bust measurement 27½ (29½, 31½, 33½, 35½, 37½)" (70 [75, 80, 85, 90, 95] cm). (**Note** Garment is designed to be a snug fit and will stretch to fit.)

Finished length from underarm 13 (13½, 13½, 13¾, 13¾, 14¼)" (33 [34, 34, 35, 35, 36] cm).

YARN

Fingering yarn (MC):

Swans Island "Fingering" (100% organic merino wool, 580 yd [530 m]/100 g): oatmeal, 1 (2, 2, 2, 2, 2) skeins.

Size 20 crochet cotton (CC):

Anchor "Freccia size 20" (100% cotton, 558 yd [510 m]/50 g): cream (6650), 1 ball.

NEEDLES

Size U.S. size 1 (2.25 mm) needles; U.S. size 2 (2.75 mm) needles; U.S. size 2/3 (3 mm) needles; one U.S. size 6 (4 mm) needle. Adjust needle size if necessary to obtain correct gauge.

NOTIONS

Remnants of same (or similar) thickness crochet cotton in contrast color for optional embroidery.

GAUGE

32 stitches and 64 rows = 4" (10 cm) in garter stitch.

ABBREVIATIONS

See page 133.

BACK

Using U.S. size 2 (2.75 mm) needles and MC, CO 103 (111, 119, 127, 135, 143) sts. Work in garter st for 10 rows. Change to U.S. size 2/3 (3 mm) needles. Cont in garter st for 14 rows, dec 1 st at each end of next row, then every 12th row 3 times—95 (103, 111, 119, 127, 135) sts. Work 5 rows, ending with a WS row.

Shape waist ribbing

Change to U.S. size 2 (2.75 mm) needles.
Next row (RS) K1, *p1, k1, rep from * to end.
Next row P1, *k1, p1, rep from * to end.
These 2 rows form rib.

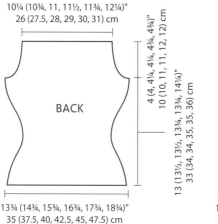

10¼ (10¾, 11, 11½, 11¾, 12¼)"
26 (27.5, 28, 29, 30, 31) cm

4 (4, 4¼, 4¼, 4¾, 4¾)"
10 (10, 11, 11, 12, 12) cm

BACK

13 (13½, 13½, 13¾, 13¾, 14¼)"
33 (34, 34, 35, 35, 36) cm

13¾ (14¾, 15¾, 16¾, 17¾, 18¾)"
35 (37.5, 40, 42.5, 45, 47.5) cm

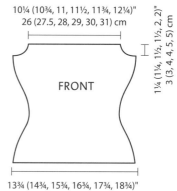

10¼ (10¾, 11, 11½, 11¾, 12¼)"
26 (27.5, 28, 29, 30, 31) cm

1¼ (1¼, 1½, 1½, 2, 2)"
3 (3, 4, 4, 5, 5) cm

FRONT

13¾ (14¾, 15¾, 16¾, 17¾, 18¾)"
35 (37.5, 40, 42.5, 45, 47.5) cm

Work in rib until back measures 4" (10 cm) from start of ribbing, ending with a WS row.

Change to U.S. size 2/3 (3 mm) needles.

Work in garter st, inc 1 st at each end of 11th row, then every 10th row 6 times—109 (117, 125, 133, 141, 149) sts. Cont without further shaping until back measures 13 (13½, 13½, 13¾, 13¾, 14¼)" (33 [34, 34, 35, 35, 36] cm), from CO edge, ending with a WS row.

Shape armholes

BO 6 (7, 7, 8, 8, 9) sts at beg of next 2 rows—97 (103, 111, 117, 125, 131) sts.

Next row K3, k2tog, knit to last 5 sts, skp, k3—2 sts dec'd.

Working all decreases as set by last row, dec 1 st at each end of every row 0 (2, 2, 4, 4, 6) times, then every other row 7 (6, 9, 8, 11, 10) times—81 (85, 87, 91, 93, 97) sts.**

Work 45 rows, ending with a WS row.

Using U.S. size 6 (4 mm) needle, BO.

FRONT

Work as given for back to **.

Work 1 row, ending with a WS row.

Using U.S. size 6 (4 mm) needle, BO.

FRONT TRIM

Using U.S. size 1 (2.25 mm) needles and CC, CO 22 sts.

Row 1 K4, yo, k1, skp, p1, k2tog, k1, yo, p1, skp, p1, k2tog, yo, k1, yo, k4.

Row 2 P8, k1, p1, k1, p3, k1, p7.

Row 3 K4, yo, k1, skp, p1, k2tog, k1, p1, sk2p, yo, k3, yo, k4—21 sts.

Row 4 P10, k1, p2, k1, p7.

Row 5 K3, [k1, yo] twice, skp, p1, [k2tog] twice, yo, k5, yo, k4—22 sts.

Row 6 P11, k1, p1, K1, p8.

Row 7 K4, yo, k3, yo, sk2p, p1, yo, k1, skp, p1, k2tog, k1, yo, k4.

Row 8 P7, k1, p3, k1, p10.

Row 9 K4, yo, k5, yo, skp, k1, skp, p1, k2tog, k1, yo, k4.

Row 10 P7, k1, p2, k1, p11.

Rep these 10 rows until trim fits neatly across BO edge of front, ending with patt Row 10 and a WS row.

BO.

FINISHING

Sew side seams. Neatly sew one edge of front trim to front BO edge.

ARMHOLE BORDERS AND SHOULDER STRAPS (Make 2)

Using U.S. size 1 (2.25 mm) needles and CC, CO 8 sts.

Row 1 Sl 1, k4, yo, k3—9 sts.

Row 2 P8, k1.

Row 3 Sl 1, k4, yo, k1, yo, k3—11 sts.

Row 4 BO 3 sts purlwise, purl to last st, k1—8 sts.

Rep these 4 rows until piece measures 15 (15, 15¾, 15¾, 16½, 16½)" (38 [38, 40, 40, 42, 42] cm), ending with patt Row 4 and a WS row.

BO.

Join CO and BO ends of strip to form a loop. Matching strip seam to top of side seam, sew straight edge of trimming to armhole edge leaving center section free to form shoulder strap.

NECK TRIM

Work as given for armhole borders and shoulder straps, making a strip that fits neatly across BO edge of back, along side of one shoulder strap, across top of front trim, and then along side of other shoulder strap, ending with patt Row 4 and a WS row.

BO.

Join CO and BO ends of strip to form a loop. Neatly sew straight edge of trim in place. If required, work a line of cross stitches in contrasting color across top of front as in photograph.

How to work cross stitch

To work a row of cross stitches (like the ones shown opposite), you will need a sewing needle and contrasting embroidery floss. It is important to make even stitches in a neat row. Use the seam as a guide.

1 On RS, make a small diagonal stitch from bottom left to top right, taking needle through back of work before making a second diagonal stitch from top left to bottom right.

2 Repeat stitches in a neat row, one stitch distance apart.

Cross-stitch variation
Work as cross stitch above, but using longer stitches that cross over at the base.

Lace rib stockings

It is easy to forget that all stockings were once hand-knitted, but if you look through any vintage knitting patterns you will find innumerable patterns for different lace-stitch stockings. These ones are knitted in the round in a simple lace rib in 3-ply wool, with the shaping at the back. They are held up with delicate silk ribbons threaded through the tops. They would also look good knitted in a bold color, as winter warmers over leggings.

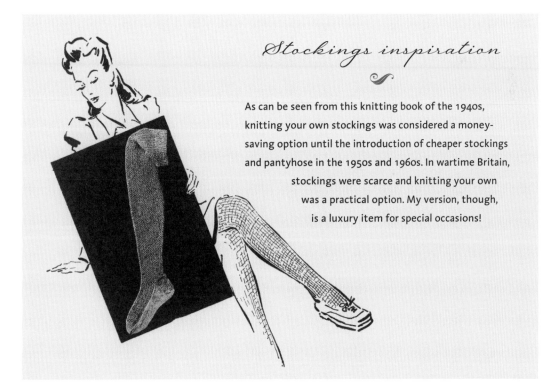

Stockings inspiration

As can be seen from this knitting book of the 1940s, knitting your own stockings was considered a money-saving option until the introduction of cheaper stockings and pantyhose in the 1950s and 1960s. In wartime Britain, stockings were scarce and knitting your own was a practical option. My version, though, is a luxury item for special occasions!

FINISHED SIZE

One size.

Length of foot (adjustable) 9" (23 cm).

YARN

Lace-weight yarn:

Patons "Fairytale Dreamtime 3-ply" (100% pure wool, 372 yd [340 m]/50 g): cream (0053), 3 balls.

NEEDLES

Set of 4 double-pointed U.S. size 2 (2.75 mm) needles (dpns); set of 4 double-pointed U.S. size 2/3 (3 mm) needles (dpns). Adjust needle size if necessary to obtain correct gauge.

NOTIONS

2 yd (1.80 m) of narrow ribbon; stitch holders.

GAUGE

32 stitches and 44 rows = 4" (10 cm) in stockinette stitch.

ABBREVIATIONS

See page 133.

STOCKINGS (Make 2)

Using U.S. size 2 (2.75 mm) dpns, CO 112 sts. Distribute sts evenly over 3 needles. Pm and join for working in rnds, being careful not to twist sts. With 4th needle, work as foll:

Rnd 1 *K1, P1, rep from * to end.

This rnd forms rib.

Work 3 more rnds in rib.

Rnd 5 (eyelet rnd) Rib 3, *yo, k2tog, rib 5, rep from * to last 4 sts, yo, k2tog, rib 2.

Work 6 rnds.

Rnd 12 K1, p1, k3tog, rib to end— 110 sts.

Work 12 rnds.

Rnd 25 K1, p3tog, rib to end— 108 sts.

Work 6 rnds.

Rnd 32 K3tog, rib to end— 106 sts.

Change to U.S. size 2/3 (3 mm) dpns.

Now work in patt as foll:

Rnd 1 [P1, k1] twice, *p2, k3, p2, k1, p1, k1, rep from * to last 2 sts, p2.

Rnd 2 [P1, k1] twice, *p2, yo, sk2p, yo, p2, k1, p1, k1, rep from * to last 2 sts, p2.

Rnd 3 As Rnd 1.

Rnd 4 [P1, k1] twice, *p2, k1, yo, skp, p2, k1, p1, k1, rep from * to last 2 sts, p2.

Rnds 5 and 6 As Rnd 1.

These 6 rnds form patt.

Work 4 rnds.

Next rnd K2tog, patt to last 3 sts, k2tog, p1— 104 sts.

Working all decreases as set by last rnd and keeping patt correct, dec 1 st at each end of every 10th rnd 8 times, then every 8th rnd 9 times— 70 sts.

Cont without further shaping until stocking measures 22½" (57 cm).

Shape heel

Break yarn.

Arrange sts for heel as foll: slip first 16 sts and last 17 sts of last round onto one dpn and leave rem 37 sts on a holder.

Working in rows, not rnds, rejoin yarn to sts on dpn and cont on this set of 33 sts only for heel as foll:

Row 1 (RS) K32, turn.

Row 2 Sl 1 purlwise, p30, turn.

Row 3 Sl 1 purlwise, k29, turn.

Row 4 Sl 1 purlwise, p28, turn.

Row 5 Sl 1 purlwise, k27, turn.

Row 6 Sl 1 purlwise, p26, turn.

Row 7 Sl 1 purlwise, k25, turn.

Row 8 Sl 1 purlwise, p24, turn.

Cont in this way, working one less st on every row before turning, until the foll row has been worked:

Row 18 Sl 1 purlwise, p14, turn.
Row 19 Sl 1 purlwise, k15, turn.
Row 20 Sl 1 purlwise, p16, turn.
Row 21 Sl 1 purlwise, k17, turn.
Row 22 Sl 1 purlwise, p18, turn.
Row 23 Sl 1 purlwise, k19, turn.
Row 24 Sl 1 purlwise, p20, turn.
Cont in this way, working one more st on every row before turning, until the foll row has been worked.
Row 36 Sl 1 purlwise, p32, turn.
These 36 rows complete heel shaping.

Shape foot
Slip 33 sts of heel and 37 sts on holder back onto dpns, distribute all 70 sts evenly and now work in rnds again as foll:
Next row (RS) K33, patt 37 sts.
Rep this rnd until work measures 7½" (19 cm) from back of heel. (Adjust length of foot here if required.)

Shape toe
Rnd 1 K1, skp, k27, k2tog, k4, skp, k27, k2tog, k3— 66 sts.
Rnd 2 Knit.
Rnd 3 K1, skp, k25, k2tog, k4, skp, k25, k2tog, k3— 62 sts.
Rnd 4 Knit.
Rnd 5 K1, skp, k23, k2tog, k4, skp, k23, k2tog, k3— 58 sts.
Rnd 6 Knit.
Rnd 7 K1, skp, k21, k2tog, k4, skp, k21, k2tog, k3— 54 sts.
Rnd 8 Knit.
Rnd 9 K1, skp, k19, k2tog, k4, skp, k19, k2tog, k3— 50 sts.
Rnd 10 Knit.
Rnd 11 K1, skp, k17, k2tog, k4, skp, k17, k2tog, k3— 46 sts.
Rnd 12 Knit.

Rnd 13 K1, skp, k15, k2tog, k4, skp, k15, k2tog, k3— 42 sts.
Rnd 14 Knit.
Rnd 15 K1, skp, k13, k2tog, k4, skp, k13, k2tog, k3— 38 sts.
Rnd 16 Knit.
Slip last st and first 18 sts of last rnd onto one dpn and rem 19 sts onto another dpn. Turn stocking inside out (with RS together) and BO both sets of 19 sts together to close toe.

FINISHING
Cut ribbon into 2 equal lengths and thread through eyelet rnd of ribbing as in photograph.

Lace shrug

The relatively low-cut sleeveless dresses of the 18th and 19th centuries, often demanded some kind of delicate covering in the evening to provide a little extra warmth. The great benefit of this little shrug, based on a Victorian "hug-me-tight," is that it makes the perfect project for someone wanting to gain experience with lace stitches, as there is no complex shaping needed and no finishing. Knitted in a baby alpaca/silk mix yarn, it is warm, light, and delicate—ideal for wearing over a flimsy dress or blouse.

Shrug inspiration

A hug-me-tight (taken from a beautifully illustrated Weldon's knitting magazine of the late 1800s), was the 19th-century equivalent of the modern shrug. The patterns, usually knitted in wool and with different stitches, were designed primarily for warmth at a time when knitted garments were mainly worn as underwear.

FINISHED SIZE

To fit bust 32– 36 (36– 40, 40– 44)" (81.5–91.5 [91.5– 101.5, 101.5– 112] cm).
Full length 19½ (21¾, 24)" (49.5 [55, 61] cm).

YARN

Lace-weight yarn:
Classic Elite "Silky Alpaca Lace" (70% alpaca, 30% silk, 440 yd [402 m]/50 g): cream (French Vanilla 2416), 2 (3, 3) balls.

NEEDLES

U.S. size 2/3 (3 mm) needles; one U.S. size 2/3 (3 mm) double-pointed needle (dpn). Adjust needle size if necessary to obtain correct gauge.

NOTIONS

Stitch holder.

ABBREVIATIONS

See page 133.

GAUGE

With yarn **DOUBLE**, 30 stitches and 40 rows = 4" (10 cm) in stockinette stitch.

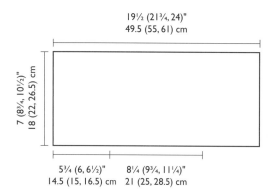

19½ (21¾, 24)"
49.5 (55, 61) cm

7 (8¾, 10½)"
18 (22, 26.5) cm

5¾ (6, 6½)"
14.5 (15, 16.5) cm

8¼ (9¾, 11¼)"
21 (25, 28.5) cm

SHRUG

Shrug is worked in one piece, starting at right underarm.

Right front

CO 58 (72, 86) sts using yarn **DOUBLE**.
Work in patt as foll:
Row 1 (RS) Sl 1 purlwise, p4, *k3, yo, k3, p8, rep from * to last 11 sts, k3, yo, k3, p4, k1 tbl—62 (77, 92) sts.
Row 2 Sl 1 purlwise, k4, *p7, k8, rep from * to last 12 sts, p7, k4, k1 tbl.
Row 3 Sl 1 purlwise, p3, *k2tog, k2, yo, k1, yo, k2, skp, p6, rep from * to last 13 sts, k2tog, k2, yo, k1, yo, k2, skp, p3, k1 tbl.
Row 4 Sl 1 purlwise, k3, *p9, k6, rep from * to last 13 sts, p9, k3, k1 tbl.
Row 5 Sl 1 purlwise, p2, *k2tog, k2, yo, k3, yo, k2, skp, p4, rep from * to last 14 sts, k2tog, k2, yo, k3, yo, k2, skp, p2, k1 tbl.
Row 6 Sl 1 purlwise, k2, *p11, k4, rep from * to last 14 sts, p11, k2, k1 tbl.
Row 7 Sl 1 purlwise, p1, *k2tog, k2, yo, k5, yo, k2, skp, p2, rep from * to last 15 sts, k2tog, k2, yo, k5, yo, k2, skp, p1, k1 tbl.
Row 8 Sl 1 purlwise, k1, *p13, k2, rep from * to last 15 sts, p13, k1, k1 tbl.
Row 9 Sl 1 purlwise, *k2tog, k2, yo, k7, yo, k2, skp, rep from * to last st, k1 tbl.
Row 10 Sl 1 purlwise, p1, psso, *p13, p2tog, rep from * to last 15 sts, p14, k1 tbl—58 (72, 86) sts.
These 10 rows form patt.
Patt 140 (150, 160) rows more—58 (72, 86) sts.

Shape back

With dpn and RS facing, pick up and knit 58 (72, 86) sts from CO edge of work. Break yarn.
Next row (RS) Patt to last 2 sts of right front, k2tog, now work across 58 (72, 86) sts on dpn as foll: k2tog, p3, *k3, yo, k3, p8, rep from * to

last 11 sts, k3, yo, k3, p4, k1 tbl—122 (152, 182) sts.

Beg with Row 2, work in patt across all sts for 109 (129, 149) rows, ending after patt Row 10 and with a WS row—116 (144, 172) sts.

Shape left front
Slip first 58 (72, 86) sts of last row (the sts above the picked-up sts) onto a holder.

Now working on just rem 58 (72, 86) sts, work in patt for 150 (160, 170) rows, ending after patt Row 10 and with a WS row—58 (72, 86) sts.
Slip sts on holder onto dpn and, taking one st from dpn with corresponding st on left needle and with RS tog, BO both sets of sts tog to form left underarm seam.

Beaded top

Beaded top inspiration ❧

This beaded georgette 1920s French frock is fastened just below the waist with a beaded sash. The elegant, narrow silhouette is typical of this period.

The 1920s saw a great change in the shape of garments from the hour-glass Edwardian form to a much simpler, more tubular shape. The design interest was created with shimmering fabrics and heavy beading. The resulting garments draped and hung beautifully. This tunic-style top has been knitted in a lustrous bamboo yarn and the beading is concentrated at the hem and neck. I used a selection of colors and sizes of beads, but the top would look good, too, with beads in a single color. Although the graphs look complex, once the position of the beads is set, they are relatively easy to follow (and, if you make the odd mistake, a few beads out of place won't matter). See also pages 72–9 for the patterns for the beaded mittens and bag.

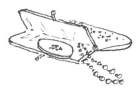

FINISHED SIZE

To fit bust 32 (34, 36, 38, 40, 42)" (81.5 [86.5, 91.5, 96.5, 101.5, 106.5] cm).

Actual bust measurement 34 (36, 38, 40, 43, 45)" (86.5 [91.5, 96.5, 101.5, 109, 114.5] cm).

Finished length 21¼ (21½, 21¾, 22¼, 22¾, 23¼)" (54 [54.5, 55, 56.5, 58, 59] cm).

YARN

Lace-weight yarn:
South West Trading "Xie" (100% bamboo, 920 yd (841 m)/100 g): grape (474), 2 (2, 2, 2, 2, 2) cones.

NEEDLES

U.S. size 3 (3.25 mm) needles; one U.S. size 8 (5 mm) needle. Adjust needle size if necessary to obtain correct gauge.

NOTIONS

Approx 1800 (1900, 2000, 2100, 2200, 2300) glass beads in a mixture of small silver-lined crystal, champagne, frosted amethyst, copper bronze metallic, matt rose, tiny crystal AB, silver-lined salmon opal and crystal; markers (m); stitch holders.

GAUGE

32 stitches and 40 rows = 4" (10 cm) in stockinette stitch.

BEADING NOTE

Before starting to knit, mix beads together so that colors and sizes will appear at random. Thread beads onto yarn by threading a fine sewing needle (one which will easily slip through beads) with sewing thread. Knot ends of thread and then pass end of yarn through this loop. Thread a bead onto sewing thread then gently slide it along and onto knitting yarn. Cont in this way until required number of beads are on yarn. To avoid damaging yarn whilst slipping beads along yarn, it is recommended that only 200 or so beads are

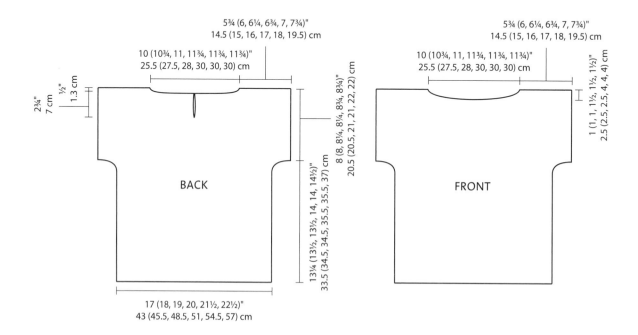

12 row patt rep

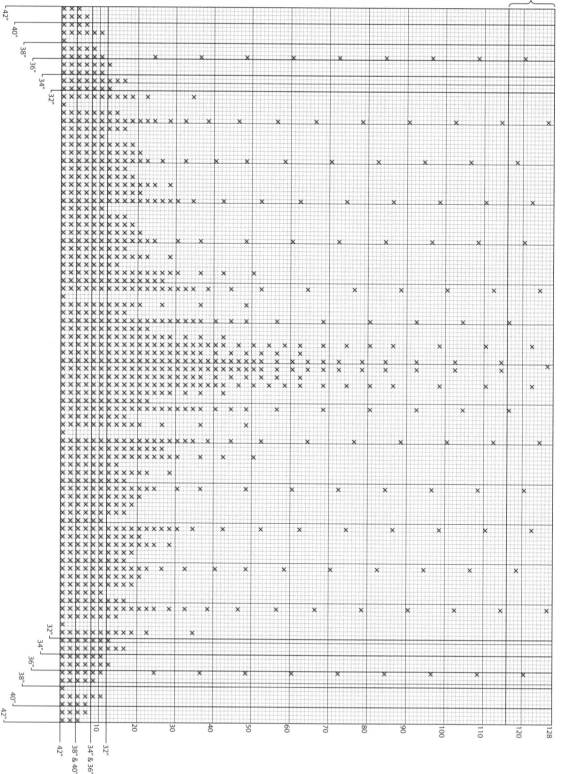

12 row patt rep

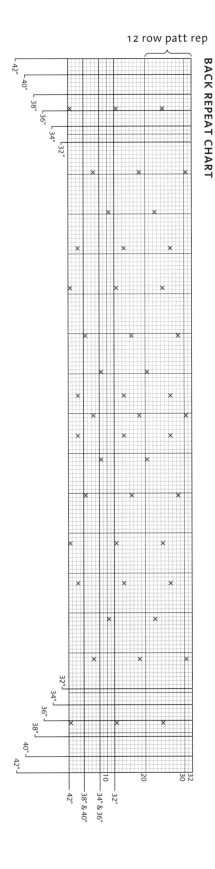

FRONT NECK MOTIF CHART

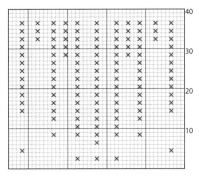

KEY

☒ Bead 1

☐ K on RS, P on WS

threaded onto yarn at one time. Once these beads have been used up, break yarn and thread more beads onto yarn before continuing.

SPECIAL ABBREVIATIONS

bead 1 = with yarn at RS of work, slip next st purlwise and slide a bead along yarn so that it sits on RS of work in front of slipped st.

See also page 133.

BACK

Using U.S. size 3 (3.25 mm) needles, CO 137 (145, 153, 161, 171, 179) sts.

Row 1 (RS) K1, *bead 1, k1, rep from * to end.

Row 2 Purl

Row 3 K2, *bead 1, k1, rep from * to end.

Row 4 Purl

Row 5 As Row 1.

Row 6 Purl.

These 6 rows complete hem edging.**

Beg and ending rows as indicated and rep the 12 row patt rep throughout, work in patt from chart for back as foll:

Work in patt until back measures 12¼ (12½, 12½, 13, 13, 13½)" (31 [32, 32, 33, 33, 34.5] cm), ending with a WS row.

Shape for sleeves

Inc 1 st at each end of next row, then every other row twice more, working inc sts into patt—143 (151, 159, 167, 177, 185) sts.

Work 1 row.

CO 3 sts at beg of next 4 rows, then 9 sts at beg of foll 2 rows—173 (181, 189, 197, 207, 215) sts.

Pm at both ends of last row.

Cont without further shaping until work measures 4¾ (4¾, 5, 5, 5½, 5½)" (12 [12, 12.5, 12.5, 14, 14] cm), from markers, ending with a WS row.

Divide for back opening

Next row (RS) Patt 86 (90, 94, 98, 103, 107) sts and turn, leaving rem 87 (91, 95, 99, 104, 108) sts on a st holder.

Work on these 86 (90, 94, 98, 103, 107) sts only for first side of neck.

Cont without further shaping until work measures 7½ (7½, 7¾, 7¾, 8¼, 8¼)" (19 [19, 19.5, 19.5, 21, 21] cm), from markers, ending with a WS row.

Shape back neck

Next row (RS) Patt 48 (50, 52, 56, 59, 63) sts and turn, leaving rem 38 (40, 42, 42, 44, 44) sts on another st holder (for back neck).

Dec 1 st at neck edge of next 2 rows—46 (48, 50, 54, 57, 61) sts.

Work 1 row, ending with a WS row.

Break yarn and leave rem sts on another holder (for right shoulder seam).

With RS tog, rejoin yarn to sts on first holder, k2tog, patt to end—86 (90, 94, 98, 103, 107) sts.

Cont without further shaping until work measures 7½ (7½, 7¾, 7¾, 8¼, 8¼)" (19 [19, 19.5, 19.5, 21, 21] cm), from markers, ending with a RS row.

Shape back neck

Next row (WS) Patt 48 (50, 52, 56, 59, 63) sts and turn, leaving rem 38 (40, 42, 42, 44, 44) sts on another st holder (for back neck).

Dec 1 st at neck edge of next 2 rows—46 (48, 50, 54, 57, 61) sts.

Work 1 row, ending with a RS row.

Break yarn and leave rem sts on another holder (for left shoulder seam).

FRONT

Work as given for back to **.

Beg and ending rows as indicated, beg your size at st and row as shown and work through Row 116 of chart—105 (108, 108, 112, 112, 116) rows of chart have been worked. Rep Rows 117–128 throughout and work as foll:

Work in patt until front matches back to start of sleeve shaping, ending with a WS row.

Shape for sleeves

Inc 1 st at each end of next row, then every other row twice more, working inc sts into patt—143 (151, 159, 167, 177, 185) sts.

Work 1 row.

CO 3 sts at beg of next 4 rows, then 9 sts at beg of foll 2 rows—173 (181, 189, 197, 207, 215) sts.

Pm at both ends of last row.

Cont in patt without further shaping until 50 (50, 50, 54, 54, 54) fewer rows have been worked than on back to sts left on shoulder holder, ending with a WS row. Pm 64 (68, 72, 76, 81, 85) sts from both ends of needle—45 sts between markers for Front Neck Motif.

Place neck motif

Next row (RS) Patt 64 (68, 72, 76, 81, 85) sts, work next 45 sts as Row 1 of Front Neck Motif chart, patt to end.

Next row Patt 64 (68, 72, 76, 81, 85) sts, work

next 45 sts as Row 2 of Front Neck Motif chart, patt to end.

These 2 rows set the sts—center 45 sts in patt from Front Neck Motif chart with sts at sides in patt as before.

Keeping sts correct as now set, work 38 rows, ending after motif chart Row 40 and with a WS row.

Shape front neck

Next row (RS) Patt 60 (62, 64, 68, 73, 77) sts and turn, leaving rem 113 (119, 125, 129, 134, 138) sts on a st holder.

Work on this set of sts only for first side of neck.

Keeping patt correct, BO 5 sts at beg of next row, then 4 sts at beg of next WS row—51 (53, 55, 59, 64, 68) sts.

Dec 1 st at neck edge of next 5 rows, then every other row 0 (0, 0, 0, 2, 2) times—46 (48, 50, 54, 57, 61) sts.

Work 1 row, ending with a WS row.

Join shoulder seam

Holding back and front with RS tog and with a U.S. size 8 (5 mm) needle, BO both sets of left shoulder sts tog.

With RS tog, slip center 53 (57, 61, 61, 61, 61) sts onto another holder, rejoin yarn to rem sts, patt to end—60 (62, 64, 68, 73, 77) sts.

Work 1 row.

Keeping patt correct, BO 5 sts at beg of next row, then 4 sts at beg of next RS row—51 (53, 55, 59, 64, 68) sts.

Dec 1 st at neck edge of next 5 rows, then on every other row 0 (0, 0, 0, 2, 2) times—46 (48, 50, 54, 57, 61) sts.

Work 1 row, ending with a RS row.

Join shoulder seam

Holding back and front with RS tog and with a

U.S. size 8 (5 mm) needle, BO both sets of right shoulder sts tog.

NECKBAND

With RS tog and U.S. size 3 (3.25 mm) needles, beg and ending at top of back opening, knit across 38 (40, 42, 42, 44, 44) sts on left back neck holder, pick up and knit 5 sts up left side of back neck, and 15 (15, 15, 19, 19, 19) sts down left side of front neck, knit across 53 (57, 61, 61, 61, 61) sts on front holder, pick up and knit 15 (15, 15, 19, 19, 19) sts up right side of front neck, and 5 sts down right side of back neck, then knit across 38 (40, 42, 42, 44, 44) sts on right back neck holder—169 (177, 185, 193, 197, 197) sts.

Row 1 (WS) Purl.

Row 2 K2, bead 1, *k3, bead 1, rep from * to last 2 sts, k2.

Using a U.S. size 8 (5 mm) needle, BO knitwise on WS.

ARMHOLE BORDERS

With RS tog and U.S. size 3 (3.25 mm) needles, pick up and knit 103 (103, 109, 109, 115, 115) sts evenly along armhole opening edge between markers.

Row 1 (WS) Purl.

Row 2 K1, *bead 1, k1, rep from * to end.

Row 3 Purl

Row 4 K2, *bead 1, k1, rep from * to last st, k1.

Using a U.S. size 8 (5 mm) needle, BO knitwise on WS. Work border along rem armhole same as first.

FINISHING

Sew side and underarm seams. At top of back opening, sew ends of neckband together.

Beaded mittens

Long, elegant gloves were de rigeur as the finishing touch to a smart outfit, particularly in the 1920s and 30s, and again in the Dior-inspired New Look of the late 1940s. Some of them were embroidered, but bead-encrusted gloves were very desirable, too. You could wear them with the beaded top on page 65, for dramatic effect, or use them to give a little black dress an extra touch of vintage glamour.

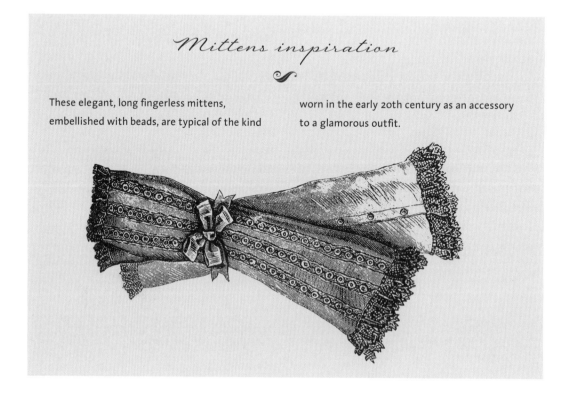

Mittens inspiration

These elegant, long fingerless mittens, embellished with beads, are typical of the kind worn in the early 20th century as an accessory to a glamorous outfit.

FINISHED SIZE
To fit an average sized woman's hand.

YARN
Lace-weight yarn:
South West Trading "Xie" (100% bamboo, 920 yd [841 m]/100 g): grape (474), 1 cone.

NEEDLES
Set of 4 double-pointed U.S. size 3 (3.25 mm) needles (dpns); one U.S. size 6 (4 mm) needle. Adjust needle size if necessary to obtain correct gauge.

NOTIONS
Approx 330 glass beads in a mixture of small silver-lined crystal, champagne and frosted amethyst, copper bronze metallic, matt rose, tiny crystal AB, silver-lined salmon opal and crystal; stitch holder.

GAUGE
32 stitches and 40 rows = 4" (10 cm) in stockinette stitch.

BEADING NOTE
Before starting to knit, mix beads together so that colors and sizes will appear at random. Thread beads onto yarn by threading a fine sewing needle (one which will easily slip through beads) with sewing thread. Knot ends of thread and then pass end of yarn through this loop. Thread a bead onto sewing thread then gently slide it along and onto knitting yarn. Cont in this way until required number of beads are on yarn. To avoid damaging yarn whilst slipping beads along yarn, it is recommended that only 200 or so beads are threaded onto yarn at one time. Once these beads have been used up, break yarn and thread more beads onto yarn before continuing.

SPECIAL ABBREVIATIONS
bead 1 = with yarn at RS of work, slip next st purlwise and slide a bead along yarn so that it sits on RS of work in front of slipped st. See also page 133.

LEFT MITT
Using U.S. size 3 (3.25 mm) dpns, CO 60 sts. Distribute sts evenly over 3 needles. Pm and join for working in rnds, being careful not to twist sts. With 4th needle, work as foll:

Rnds 1 and 2 Knit.

Work in beaded patt as foll:

Rnd 3 K10, bead 1, k49.

Rnd 4 Knit.

Rnd 5 K38, bead 1, k21.

Rnd 6 Knit.

Rnd 7 K49, bead 1, k10.

Rnd 8 Knit.

Rnd 9 K21, bead 1, k38.

Rnd 10 Knit.

Rnd 11 K30, bead 1, k29.

Rnd 12 Knit.

Rnd 13 K42, bead 1, k17.

Rnd 14 Knit.

Rnds 3 to 14 form beaded patt.

Work in patt until mitt measures 6" (15 cm).

Next rnd K1, k2tog, patt to last 3 sts, skp, k1—58 sts.

Work 11 rnds.

Rep last 12 rnds 4 times more, then rep dec rnd once more—48 sts.

Cont without further shaping until mitt measures 19" (48.5 cm).

Shape thumb gussett
Rnd 1 Patt 10 sts, yo, k2, yo, patt to end—50 sts.

Work 1 rnd even.

Rnd 3 Patt 10 sts, yo, k4, yo, patt to end—52 sts.

Work 1 rnd even.

Rnd 5 Patt 10 sts, yo, k6, yo, patt to end—54 sts.

Work 1 rnd even.

Rnd 7 Patt 10 sts, yo, k8, yo, patt to end—56 sts.

Work 1 rnd even.

Rnd 9 Patt 10 sts, yo, k10, yo, patt to end—58 sts.

Work 1 rnd even.

Rnd 11 Patt 10 sts, yo, k12, yo, patt to end—60 sts.

Work 1 rnd even.

Rnd 13 Patt 10 sts, yo, k14, yo, patt to end—62 sts.

Work 11 rnds even.

Rnd 25 Patt 10 sts, slip next 16 sts onto a holder (for thumb), turn, and CO 4 sts, turn and patt to end—50 sts.

Shape hand

Work 13 rnds.

Next rnd *Bead 1, k1, rep from * to end.

Next rnd Knit.

Next rnd *K1, bead 1, rep from * to end.

Using U.S. size 6 (4 mm) needle, BO.

Shape thumb

Slip 16 sts from holder onto dpns.

With 4th needle, work as foll:

Next rnd K16, pick up and knit 4 sts from CO sts of hand— 20 sts.

Distribute sts evenly over 3 needles. Pm and join for working in the rnd.

Knit 10 rnds.

Next rnd *Bead 1, k1, rep from * to end.

Next rnd Knit.

Next rnd *K1, bead 1, rep from * to end.

Using U.S. size 6 (4 mm) needle, BO.

RIGHT MITT

Work as given for left mitt to start of thumb gusset shaping.

Shape thumb gussett

Rnd 1 Patt 36 sts, yo, k2, yo, patt to end—50 sts.

Work 1 rnd even.

Rnd 3 Patt 36 sts, yo, k4, yo, patt to end—52 sts.

Work 1 rnd even.

Rnd 5 Patt 36 sts, yo, k6, yo, patt to end—54 sts.

Work 1 rnd even.

Rnd 7 Patt 36 sts, yo, k8, yo, patt to end—56 sts.

Work 1 rnd even.

Rnd 9 Patt 36 sts, yo, k10, yo, patt to end—58 sts.

Work 1 rnd even.

Rnd 11 Patt 36 sts, yo, k12, yo, patt to end—60 sts.

Work 1 rnd even.

Rnd 13 Patt 36 sts, yo, k14, yo, patt to end—62 sts.

Work 11 rnds even.

Rnd 25 Patt 36 sts, slip next 16 sts onto a holder (for thumb), turn, and CO 4 sts, turn and patt to end—50 sts.

Complete as given for left mitt from start of hand shaping.

Beaded bag

If you are not expert at knitting with beads, you might like to make a start with this chic beaded bag. Knitted in firm Fabric stitch, it doesn't require a lining. You could make it in a color to match a favorite outfit. Although the metal frames can be bought new, I took one from an old retro style bag found in a flea market, giving my version an authentic vintage look.

Beaded bag inspiration

This 19th-century chain-mail bag with its ornate frame, is the type of smart evening bag that inspired my version.

FINISHED SIZE

Completed bag is 6" (15 cm) wide and 5" (12.5 cm) deep.

YARN

Lace-weight yarn:
South West Trading "Xie" (100% bamboo, 920 yd [841 m]/100 g): grape (474), 1 cone.

NEEDLES

U.S. size 6 (4 mm) needles. Adjust needle size if necessary to obtain correct gauge.

NOTIONS

Approx 700 glass beads in a mixture of small silver-lined crystal, champagne and frosted amethyst, copper bronze metallic, matt rose, tiny crystal AB, silver-lined salmon opal and crystal; metal purse frame 4¾" (12 cm) wide.

GAUGE

With yarn **DOUBLE**, 37 stitches and 60 rows = 4" (10 cm) in pattern.

BEADING NOTE

Before starting to knit, mix beads together so that colors and sizes will appear at random. Thread beads onto yarn by threading a fine sewing needle (one which will easily slip through beads) with sewing thread. Knot ends of thread and then pass end of yarn through this loop. Thread a bead onto sewing thread then gently slide it along and onto knitting yarn. Cont in this way until required number of beads are on yarn. To avoid damaging yarn whilst slipping beads along yarn, it is recommended that only 200 or so beads are threaded onto yarn at one time. Once these beads have been used up, break yarn and thread more beads onto yarn before continuing.

Note Yarn is used **DOUBLE** throughout so beads need to be threaded onto doubled yarn.

SPECIAL ABBREVIATIONS

bead 1 = with yarn at RS of work, slip next st purlwise and slide a bead along yarn so that it sits on RS of work in front of slipped st. See also page 133.

BAG

Using U.S. size 6 (4 mm) needles and yarn **DOUBLE**, CO 55 sts.
Row 1 (RS) K1, *slip next st with yarn at front (RS) of work, k1, rep from * to end.
Row 2 K1, p1, *slip next st with yarn at back (RS) of work, p1, rep from * to last st, k1.
These 2 rows form patt.
Keeping patt correct, now work from chart as foll:
Work chart rows 1–10 three times.
Work chart rows 11–46 once.
Work chart rows 47–48 fifteen times.
Work chart rows 49–84 once.
Work chart rows 85–94 three times.
BO.

FINISHING

Sew knitted section to bag frame, then sew side seams.

BEAD CHART

work 3 times

KEY

⊠ Bead 1

☐ K on RS, P on WS

work 15 times

work 3 times

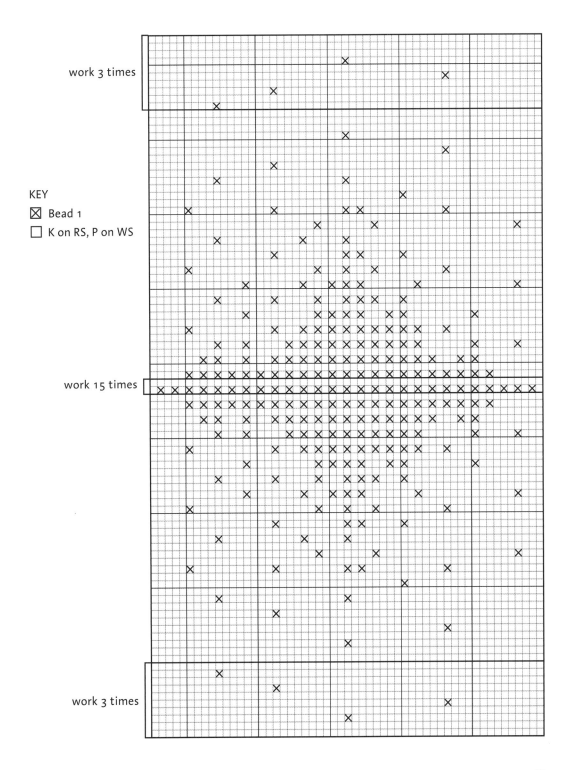

Lace blouse

Some of the prettiest garments have the simplest shapes, like this little 1930s-inspired lace blouse knitted in silky crochet cotton. It has a plain stockinette stitch back and a lace stitch front. The design interest and shaping are created by a couple of simple pleats at the front waist, and a tie belt at the back, avoiding any complicated shaping on the lace pattern itself. There is a crochet edging around the fronts and the collar, and some pretty vintage glass buttons providing a finishing touch.

Lace blouse inspiration

Figure-hugging pretty lacy tops like this one are typical of the late 1930s and early 40s, and the pattern books of the period have any number to choose from, many knitted in fine yarns with textured or lacy stitch patterns.

FINISHED SIZE

To fit bust 32 (34, 36, 38, 40, 42)" (81.5 [86.5, 91.5, 96.5, 101.5, 106.5] cm).

Actual bust measurement 33½ (35¼, 37¼, 39¼, 41¼, 43¾)" (85 [89.5, 94.5, 99.5, 105, 111] cm).

Finished length 19¼ (19¾, 20, 20½, 21, 21½)" (49 [50, 51, 52, 53.5, 54.5] cm).

YARN

Size 12 crochet cotton:

Anchor "Pellicano" (100% cotton, 421 yd [385 m]/50 g): ecru (12), 3 (3, 3, 4, 4, 4) balls.

NEEDLES AND CROCHET HOOK

U.S. size 1 (2.25 mm) needles ; U.S. size 2 (2.75 mm) needles; U.S. size 3 (3.25 mm) needles; U.S. size 5 (3.75 mm) needles; U.S. size 1 steel (2 mm) crochet hook. Adjust needle size if necessary to obtain correct gauge.

NOTIONS

Markers (m); 8 small glass buttons, ½" (13 mm) diameter; sewing needle and thread (for sewing on buttons).

GAUGE

37 stitches and 47 rows = 4" (10 cm) in stockinette stitch.

37 stitches and 54 rows = 4" (10 cm) in lace pattern.

ABBREVIATIONS

See page 133.

Crochet instructions use U.S. terms, see page 133 for U.K. equivalents.

BACK

Using U.S. size 2 (2.75 mm) needles, CO 145 (153, 163, 171, 181, 189) sts.

Rows 1–4 Knit.

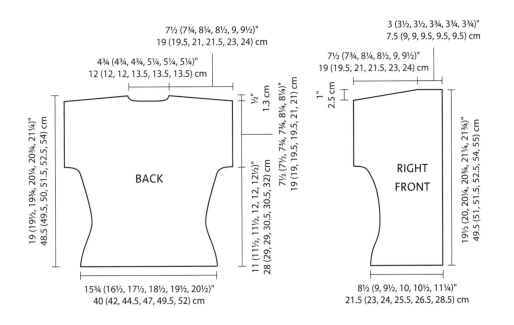

BACK

7½ (7¾, 8¼, 8½, 9, 9½)"
19 (19.5, 21, 21.5, 23, 24) cm

4¾ (4¾, 4¾, 5¼, 5¼, 5¼)"
12 (12, 12, 13.5, 13.5, 13.5) cm

½"
1.3 cm

7½ (7½, 7¾, 7¾, 8¼, 8¼)"
19 (19, 19.5, 19.5, 21, 21) cm

19 (19½, 19¾, 20¼, 20¾, 21¼)"
48.5 (49.5, 50, 51.5, 52.5, 54) cm

11 (11½, 11½, 12, 12, 12½)"
28 (29, 29, 30.5, 30.5, 32) cm

15¾ (16½, 17½, 18½, 19½, 20½)"
40 (42, 44.5, 47, 49.5, 52) cm

RIGHT FRONT

3 (3½, 3½, 3¾, 3¾, 3¾)"
7.5 (9, 9, 9.5, 9.5, 9.5) cm

7½ (7¾, 8¼, 8½, 9, 9½)"
19 (19.5, 21, 21.5, 23, 24) cm

1"
2.5 cm

19½ (20, 20¼, 20¾, 21¼, 21¾)"
49.5 (51, 51.5, 52.5, 54, 55) cm

8½ (9, 9½, 10, 10½, 11¼)"
21.5 (23, 24, 25.5, 26.5, 28.5) cm

Beg with a RS row, work in St st throughout as foll:

Work 20 rows.

Counting in from both ends of last row, pm after 48th (51st, 54th, 57th, 60th, 63rd) st from each end of row—there should be 49 (51, 55, 57, 61, 63) sts between markers.

Next row (RS) K1, k2tog, [knit to 3 sts before m, k2tog, k2 (m is between these 2 sts), skp] twice, knit to last 3 sts, skp, k1—139 (147, 157, 165, 175, 183) sts.

Work 7 rows even.

Rep last 8 rows twice more, then rep dec row once more—121 (147, 157, 165, 175, 183) sts.

Work 17 rows even.

Next row (RS) K1, M1, [knit to 1 st before m, M1, k2 (m is between these 2 sts), M1] twice, knit to last st, M1, k1—127 (135, 145, 153, 163, 171) sts.

Work 7 rows even.

Rep last 8 rows twice more, then rep inc row once more—145 (153, 163, 171, 181, 189) sts.

Cont without further shaping until back measures 10½ (11, 11, 11½, 11½, 12)" (26.5 [28, 28, 29, 29, 30,5] cm), ending with a WS row.

Shape for sleeves

CO 6 sts at beg of next 6 rows—181 (189, 199, 207, 217, 225) sts.

Pm at both ends of last row.

Cont without further shaping until work measures 7½ (7½, 7¾, 7¾, 8¼, 8¼)" (19 [19, 19.5, 19.5, 21, 21] cm), from m, ending with a WS row.

Shape shoulders and back neck

Next row (RS) K71 (74, 79, 81, 86, 90), k2tog, and turn.

Next row P48 (50, 53, 54, 58, 60) and turn.

Next row Knit to last 2 sts, k2tog.

Next row P24 (25, 26 27, 29, 30) and turn.

Next row Knit to last 2 sts, k2tog.

Using U.S. size 5 (3.75 mm) needles, BO 69 (72, 77, 79, 84, 88) sts purlwise.

With RS facing and U.S. size 5 (3.75 mm) needles, rejoin yarn to rem sts, BO center 37 (39, 39, 43, 43, 43) sts, then with U.S. size 2 (2.75 mm) needles knit to end—72 (75, 80, 82, 87, 91) sts rem.

Next row (WS) Purl to last 2 sts, p2tog.

Next row K48 (50, 53, 54, 58, 60) and turn.

Next row Purl to last 2 sts, p2tog.

Next row K24 (25, 26, 27, 29, 30) and turn.

Next row Purl to last 2 sts, p2tog.

Using U.S. size 5 (3.75 mm) needles, BO rem 69 (72, 77, 79, 84, 88) sts knitwise.

LEFT FRONT

Using U.S. size 1 (2.25 mm) needles, CO 78 (83, 88, 93, 98, 103) sts.

Work in lace patt as foll:

Row 1 (RS) K1, *k1, yo, k3, sk2p, k3, yo, rep from * to last 7 (2, 7, 2, 7, 2) sts, [k1, yo, k3, skp] 1 (0, 1, 0, 1, 0) time(s), k1 (2, 1, 2, 1, 2).

Row 2 Purl.

Row 3 K1, *k2, yo, k2, sk2p, k2, yo, k1, rep from * to last 7 (2, 7, 2, 7, 2) sts, [k2, yo, k2, skp] 1 (0, 1, 0, 1, 0) time(s), k1 (2, 1, 2, 1, 2).

Row 4 Purl.

Row 5 K1, k2tog, yo, *k1, yo, k1, sk2p, [k1, yo] twice, sk2p, yo, rep from * to last 5 (10, 5, 10, 5, 10) sts, [k1, yo, k1, skp] 1 (0, 1, 0, 1, 0) time(s), [k1, yo, k1, sk2p, k1, yo, k1, yo, skp] 0 (1, 0, 1, 0, 1) time(s), k1.

Row 6 Purl.

These 6 rows form patt.

Cont in patt for 36 rows more, ending with a WS row.

Shape pleat

Next row (RS) Patt 37 (42, 47, 42, 47, 52) sts, BO next 10 sts, patt to end—68 (73, 78, 83, 88, 93) sts.

Work 53 rows even.

Next row (RS) Patt 37 (42, 47, 42, 47, 52) sts, turn and CO 10 sts, turn and patt to end—78 (83, 88, 93, 98, 103) sts.

Cont without further shaping until left front matches back to beg of sleeve shaping, ending with a WS row.

Shape for sleeve

Keeping patt correct, CO 6 sts at beg of next 2 RS rows, then 8 sts at beg of next RS row —98 (103, 108, 113, 118, 123) sts.

Pm at beg of last row.

Cont without further shaping until left front matches back to beg of shoulder shaping, ending with a RS row.

Shape shoulder

Next row (WS) P88 (93, 98, 103, 108, 113) and turn.

Next row Work in patt to end.

Next row P78 (83, 88, 93, 98, 103) and turn.

Next row Work in patt to end.

Next row P68 (73, 78, 83, 88, 93) and turn.

Next row Work in patt to end.

Next row P58 (63, 68, 73, 78, 83) and turn.

Next row Work in patt to end.

Next row P48 (53, 58, 63, 68, 73) and turn.

Next row Work in patt to end.

Next row P38 (43, 48, 53, 58, 63) and turn.

Next row Work in patt to end.

Sizes 39¼" (99.5 cm), 41¼" (105 cm), and 43¾" (111 cm) only

Next row P(43, 48, 53) and turn.

Next row Work in patt to end.

All sizes

Using U.S. size 3 (3.25 mm) needles, BO all 98 (103, 108, 113, 118, 123) sts purlwise.

RIGHT FRONT

Using U.S. size 1 (2.25 mm) needles, CO 78 (83, 88, 93, 98, 103) sts.

To form pleats

To create the shaping detail at the waist, you need to form a pleat at each bound-off and cast-on edge, hand-stitched in place.

1 Fold the top and bottom of each pleat to WS and pin in place to form box pleat on WS.

2 On RS, with a needle and matching yarn, oversew each inverted pleat in place with a few long hand-stitches.

Work in lace patt as foll:

Row 1 (RS) K1, [k2tog, k3, yo] 1 (0, 1, 0, 1, 0) time(s), *k1, yo, k3, sk2p, k3, yo, rep from * to last 2 sts, k2.

Row 2 Purl.

Row 3 K1, [k2tog, k2, yo, k1] 1 (0, 1, 0, 1, 0) time(s), *k2, yo, k2, sk2p, k2, yo, k1, rep from * to last 2 sts, k2.

Row 4 Purl.

Row 5 [K1, k2tog, k1, yo, k1] 1 (0, 1, 0, 1, 0) time(s), [k1, k2tog, yo, k1, yo, k1, sk2p, k1, yo, K1] 0 (1, 0, 1, 0, 1) time(s), *yo, sk2p, [yo, k1] twice, sk2p, k1, yo, k1, rep from * to last 3 sts, yo, skp, k1.

Row 6 Purl.

These 6 rows form patt.

Cont in patt for 36 rows more, ending with a WS row.

Shape pleat

Next row (RS) Patt 31 (31, 31, 41, 41, 41) sts, BO next 10 sts, patt to end—68 (73, 78, 83, 88, 93) sts.

Work 53 rows even.

Next row (RS) Patt 31 (31, 31, 41, 41, 41) sts, turn and CO 10 sts, turn and patt to end—78 (83, 88, 93, 98, 103) sts.

Cont without further shaping until right front matches back to beg of sleeve shaping, ending with a RS row.

Shape for sleeve

Keeping patt correct, CO 6 sts at beg of next 2 WS rows, then 8 sts at beg of next WS row —98 (103, 108, 113, 118, 123) sts.

Pm at beg of last row.

Cont without further shaping until right front matches back to beg of shoulder shaping, ending with a RS row.

Shape shoulder

Next row (RS) Patt 88 (93, 98, 103, 108, 113) sts and turn.

Next row Purl.

Next row Patt 78 (83, 88, 93, 98, 103) sts and turn.

Next row Purl.

Next row Patt 68 (73, 78, 83, 88, 93) sts and turn.

Next row Purl.

Next row Patt 58 (63, 68, 73, 78, 83) sts and turn.

Next row Purl.

Next row Patt 48 (53, 58, 63, 68, 73) sts and turn.

Next row Purl.

Next row Patt 38 (43, 48, 53, 58, 63) sts and turn.

Next row Purl.

Sizes 39¼" (99.5 cm), 41¼" (105 cm), and 43¾" (111 cm) only

Next row Patt (43, 48, 53) sts and turn.

Next row Purl.

All sizes

Using U.S. size 3 (3.25 mm) needles, BO all 98 (103, 108, 113, 118, 123) sts knitwise.

TIES (Make 2)

Using U.S. size 1 (2.25 mm) needles, CO 12 sts.

Row 1 [K1, p1] 6 times.

Rep this row until tie measures 19½ (20, 20½, 21, 21½, 22)" (49.5 [51, 52, 53.5, 54.5, 56] cm). BO.

FINISHING

At base of front pleats, fold BO sts to form a pleat on WS and over sew in place as in photograph. In same way, fold CO edge at top of pleat to form a pleat and sew in place. Sew side and underarm seams below markers, inserting one end of tie into side seam 4" (10 cm) up from CO edge. Sew shoulder seams. Mark positions for 8 button loops along right front opening edge—first to come just above CO edge, last to come 5 (5, 5, 5½, 5½, 5½)" (12.5 [12.5, 12.5, 14,

14, 14] cm), down from BO edge, and rem 6 button loops evenly spaced between.

EDGING

With RS facing and U.S. size 1 steel (2 mm) crochet hook, attach yarn at base of right front opening edge, ch 1 (does NOT count as st), work 1 row of sc evenly up right front opening edge, around entire neck edge, and down left front opening edge to CO edge, turn.

Next row Ch 1 (does NOT count as st), 1 sc into each sc to end, working 3 sc into front neck corner points and skipping sc as required around neck edge to ensure edging lays flat, turn.

Rep last row twice more, ensuring number of sts in last row is divisible by 3.

Next row Ch 1 (does NOT count as st), 1 sc into first sc, ch 10 (to form first button loop), skip 1 sc, 1 sc into each of next 2 sc, *ch 4, skip 1 sc, 1 sc into each of next 2 sc, rep from * to last 2 sts, replacing the (ch 4) with (ch 10) at each marked button loop position, ch 4, skip 1 sc, 1 sc into last sc.

Fasten off.

Sew on buttons to correspond with button loops.

Lace gloves

Gloves have long been the finishing touch to an outfit and up until the early 1950s no lady worth her salt would be seen out without a pair. Lace gloves, though, were particularly popular in the early 20th century. These ones are knitted in a simple open mesh pattern, with a pretty border added afterward. I've used green glass vintage buttons on these to give a unique finishing touch. They would be perfect for a wedding or formal occasion.

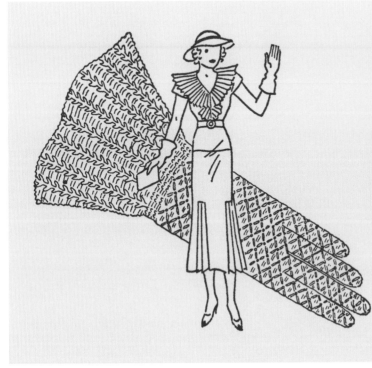

Lace glove inspiration

These lace gloves with a deep cuff, take their inspiration from images like this one from the late 1930s, when lace gloves were the perfect addition to a summer outfit.

FINISHED SIZE
To fit an average sized woman's hand.

YARN
Size 12 crochet cotton:
Anchor "Pellicano" (100% cotton, 421 yd [385 m]/50 g]: ecru (12), 1 ball.

NEEDLES
U.S. size 2/3 (3 mm) needles; U.S. size 1 (2.25 mm) needles. Adjust needle size if necessary to obtain correct gauge.

NOTIONS
2 glass buttons, ¾" (19 mm) diameter; sewing needle and thread (for sewing on buttons).

GAUGE
28 stitches and 40 rows = 4" (10 cm) over lace pattern.

ABBREVIATIONS
See page 133.

FIRST GLOVE
Using U.S. size 2/3 (3 mm) needles, CO 42 sts.
Knit one row.
Work in patt throughout as foll:
Row 1 (RS) *K1, yo, k2tog, rep from * to end.
Row 2 As Row 1.
Last 2 rows form patt.
Work in patt for 2 rows more.

Shape thumb gussett
Row 1 (RS) Patt 21 sts, yo, k1, yo, k2tog, patt 18 sts—43 sts.
Row 2 Patt 18 sts, [k1, yo] twice, k2tog, patt 21 sts—44 sts.
Row 3 Patt 21 sts, k1, yo, k2, yo, k2tog, patt 18 sts—45 sts.
Work 3 rows even.

Row 7 Patt 21 sts, yo, k1, yo, k2tog, patt 21 sts—46 sts.
Row 8 Patt 18 sts, [k1, yo] twice, k2tog, patt 24 sts—47 sts.
Row 9 Patt 21 sts, k1, yo, k2, yo, k2tog, patt 21 sts—48 sts.
Work 3 rows even.
Row 13 Patt 24 sts, yo, k1, yo, k2tog, patt 21 sts—49 sts.
Row 14 Patt 21 sts, [k1, yo] twice, k2tog, patt 24 sts—50 sts.
Row 15 Patt 24 sts, k1, yo, k2, yo, k2tog, patt 21 sts—51 sts.
Work 9 rows even, ending with a WS row.

Shape thumb
Next row (RS) Patt 33 sts and turn.
Next row CO 3 sts, patt across these 3 sts, patt next 12 sts, and turn.
Work 22 rows on these 15 sts only.
Next row (RS) [K1, k2tog] 5 times—10 sts.
Next row [K2tog] 5 times.
Break yarn and thread through rem 5 sts. Pull up tight and fasten off securely.
Sew thumb seam.

Shape hand
With RS facing, pick up and knit 3 sts from CO edge at base of thumb, patt to end—42 sts.
Work 13 rows, ending with a WS row.

Shape index finger
Next row (RS) Patt 27 sts and turn.
Next row CO 3 sts, patt across these 3 sts, patt next 12 sts, and turn.
Work 28 rows on these 15 sts only.
Next row (RS) [K1, k2tog] 5 times—10 sts.
Next row [K2tog] 5 times.
Break yarn and thread through rem 5 sts. Pull up tight and fasten off securely.
Sew finger seam.

Shape middle finger

With RS facing, pick up and knit 3 sts from CO edge at base of index finger, k1, yo, k2tog, k1, yo, k1, and turn.

Next row (WS) Patt 9 sts, k1, yo, k2tog, k1, yo, k1, and turn.

Work 32 rows on these 15 sts only.

Next row (RS) [K1, k2tog] 5 times—10 sts.

Next row [K2tog] 5 times.

Break yarn and thread through rem 5 sts. Pull up tight and fasten off securely.

Sew finger seam.

Shape ring finger

With RS facing, pick up and knit 3 sts from base of middle finger, k2, yo, k2tog, k1, and turn.

Next row CO 2 sts, patt across these 2 sts, patt next 13 sts and turn.

Work 28 rows on these 15 sts only.

Next row (RS) [K1, k2tog] 5 times—10 sts.

Next row [K2tog] 5 times.

Break yarn and thread through rem 5 sts. Pull up tight and fasten off securely.

Sew finger seam.

Shape little finger

With RS facing, pick up and knit 2 sts from base of ring finger, yo, k2tog, k1, yo, k2tog, turn.

Next row Patt 7 sts, then patt across rem 5 sts and turn.

Work 25 rows on these 12 sts only.

Next row (RS) [K1, k2tog] 4 times—8 sts.

Next row [K2tog] 4 times.

Break yarn and thread through rem 4 sts. Pull up tight and fasten off securely.

Sew finger seam, continuing down side of hand to a point 1½" (4 cm) up from CO edge.

SECOND GLOVE

Work as given for first glove, reading RS for WS and vice versa and reversing seams—fabric is reversible.

CUFFS (Make 2)

Using U.S. size 1 (2.25 mm) needles, CO 17 sts.

Knit one row.

Now work in patt as foll:

Row 1 (RS) K3, [yo, p2tog] twice, yo, k1 tbl, k2tog, p1, skp, k1 tbl, yo, k3.

Row 2 K3, p3, k1, p3, k2, [yo, p2tog] twice, k1.

Rows 3 and 4 As Rows 1 and 2.

Row 5 K3, [yo, p2tog] twice, yo, k1 tbl, yo, k2tog, p1, skp, yo, k4—18 sts.

Row 6 K4, p2, k1, p4, k2, [yo, p2tog] twice, k1.

Row 7 K3, [yo, p2tog] twice, yo, k1 tbl, k1, k1 tbl, yo, sk2p, yo, k5—19 sts.

Row 8 K5, p7, k2, [yo, p2tog] twice, k1.

Row 9 K3, [yo, p2tog] twice, yo, k1 tbl, k3, k1 tbl, yo, k7—21 sts.

Row 10 BO 4 sts (one st on right needle), k2, p7, k2, [yo, p2tog] twice, k1—17 sts.

Rep these 10 rows 10 times more.

BO.

FINISHING

Sew straight edge of cuff to CO edge of glove.

OPENING EDGING

With RS facing, pick up and knit 20 sts down one side of opening, then 20 sts up other side of opening—40 sts.

BO.

Make button loop and attach button to opening edging even with cuff seam.

Zigzag bag

Zigzag bag inspiration

❧

The shape of this little fabric drawstring bag inspired my own crochet version. It was taken from *Stitchery*, an early 20th-century home-crafts book, which included the instructions for making it.

Little drawstring bags were popular in the 18th and 19th centuries to hold a dance card and some hair pins, but the colors and patterns of this particular one are inspired by the 1930s. The simple lace stitch in colorful crochet cotton, gives the effective zigzag pattern. The drawstring handles can be worn around the wrist, making it a great way to carry a few essentials when nothing more formal is required. Knitted in cream silk, it would be ideal for a bride.

FINISHED SIZE

Completed bag is 5¼" (13.5 cm) tall (measured from top of base) and 8¾" (22 cm) all round.

YARN

Size 8 pearl cotton:
DMC "Pearl Cotton no 8" (100% cotton, 95 yd [87 m]/10 g): 1 ball in each of green (Nile Green 913), cream (Ecru), orange (Bright Orange 608), peach (Tawny 945), and brown (Coffee Brown 938).

NEEDLES AND CROCHET HOOK

U.S. size 0 (2 mm) needles: one pair straight needles and one set of 4 double-pointed needles (dpns); U.S. size 7 steel (1.50 mm) crochet hook. Adjust needle size if necessary to obtain correct gauge.

GAUGE

57 stitches and 54 rows = 4" (10 cm) in zigzag pattern.

ABBREVIATIONS

See page 133.

BAG

Bag is worked from top downward. Zigzag section is worked in rows, then base is worked in rnds.
Using U.S. size 0 (2 mm) needles and green, CO 135 sts.
Knit one row.
Now work in zigzag patt as foll:

Row 1 (RS) K1, skp, *k9, s2kp, rep from * to last 12 sts, k9, k2tog, k1.

Row 2 K1, *p1, k4, [k1, yo, k1] all into next st, k4, rep from * to last 2 sts, p1, k1.

Break off green and join in cream.

Row 3 As Row 1.

Row 4 P6, *[k1, yo, k1] all into next st, p9, rep from * to last 7 sts, [k1, yo, k1] all into next st, p6.

Rows 5 to 20 As Rows 3 and 4, 8 times.

Row 21 (eyelet row) K1, skp, *k4, yo, k2tog, k3, s2kp, rep from * to last 12 sts, k4, yo, k2tog, k3, k2tog, k1.

Row 22 As Row 4.

Now joining in and breaking off colors as required, cont in patt in stripes as foll:

Rows 23 and 24 Using orange, as Rows 1 and 2.

Rows 25 to 28 Using peach, as Rows 3 and 4 twice.

Rows 29 to 32 Using brown, as Rows 1 and 2 twice.

Rows 33 to 38 Using green, as Rows 3 and 4 three times.

Rows 39 and 40 Using cream, as Rows 3 and 4.

Rows 41 and 42 Using orange, as Rows 1 and 2.

Rows 43 to 48 Using peach, as Rows 3 and 4 three times.

Rows 49 to 54 Using brown, as Rows 3 and 4 three times.

Rows 55 to 58 Using green, as Rows 3 and 4 twice.

Rows 59 to 62 Using cream, as Rows 3 and 4 twice.

Rows 63 and 64 Using orange, as Rows 1 and 2.

Rows 65 to 68 Using peach, as Rows 3 and 4 twice.

Rows 69 and 70 Using brown, as Rows 1 and 2.

Rows 71 to 74 Using green, as Rows 3 and 4 twice.

Rows 75 and 76 Using cream, as Rows 1 and 2.

Rows 77 and 78 Using orange, as Rows 1 and 2.

Rows 79 and 80 Using peach, as Rows 3 and 4.

These 80 rows complete zigzag section.

Shape base

Break off contrast colors and cont using brown only.
Distribute sts evenly over 3 of the 4 dpns. Pm

and join for working in rnds. Using 4th dpn, work in rnds as foll:

Rnds 1 and 2 (RS) Knit.

Rnd 3 [K12, sk2p, k12] 5 times— 125 sts.

Rnds 4 and 5 Knit.

Rnd 6 [K11, sk2p, k11] 5 times— 115 sts.

Rnds 7 and 8 Knit.

Rnd 9 [K10, sk2p, k10] 5 times— 105 sts.

Rnds 10 and 11 Knit.

Rnd 12 [K9, sk2p, k9] 5 times—95 sts.

Rnds 13 and 14 Knit.

Rnd 15 [K8, sk2p, k8] 5 times—85 sts.

Rnds 16 and 17 Knit.

Rnd 18 [K7, sk2p, k7] 5 times—75 sts.

Rnds 19 and 20 Knit.

Rnd 21 [K6, sk2p, k6] 5 times—65 sts.

Rnds 22 and 23 Knit.

Rnd 24 [K5, sk2p, k5] 5 times—55 sts.

Rnds 25 and 26 Knit.

Rnd 27 [K4, sk2p, k4] 5 times—45 sts.

Rnds 28 and 29 Knit.

Rnd 30 [K3, sk2p, k3] 5 times—35 sts.
Break yarn and thread through rem 35 sts.
Pull up tight and fasten off securely.

FINISHING
Neatly sew row-end edges together above base.

TIE
With U.S. size 7 steel (1.50 mm) crochet hook, make a length of ch 31½" (80 cm) long and fasten off.
Thread tie through eyelet holes of eyelet row twice and join ends. To close bag, pull on tie at opposite sides.

Sailor-collar blouse

The Edwardian period in the early 20th century is noted for the decorative finishes added to women's clothing. I love the pretty, fine cotton-lawn blouses of this period, with their lace inserts, pintucks, and delicate embroidery, especially when combined with the elegance of the simplified silhouette of the early 1930s.

I have recreated the look using a fine crochet cotton and a variety of simple lace stitches. The main part of the blouse is knitted sideways from cuff to cuff, with a front insert and a sailor collar. The blouse looks intricate but is, in fact, not difficult to knit.

Sailor-collar blouse inspiration

Soft, flowing lines, delicate fabrics that drape well, pastel colors, and a concentration on detail, are hallmarks of the blouses and frocks of the early 20th century, often worn with long strings of beads to show off the necklines. The effect is simultaneously feminine and elegant.

FINISHED SIZE

To fit bust 32 (34, 36, 38, 40, 42)" (81.5 [86.5, 91.5, 96.5, 101.5, 106.5] cm).

Finished width (laid flat) 21 (22, 23, 24, 25, 26)" (53.5 [56, 58.5, 61, 63.5, 66] cm).

Finished length 16¾ (17¼, 17¾, 18¼, 18¾, 19)" (42.5 [44, 45, 46.5, 47.5, 48.5] cm).

Sleeve length 9½ (9½, 10, 10, 10½, 10½)" (24 [24, 25.5, 25.5, 26.5, 26.5] cm).

YARN

Size 20 mercerized crochet cotton: Anchor "Freccia 20" (100% cotton, 558 yd [510 m]/50 g): pink (0075), 4 (4, 4, 5, 5, 5) balls; white (7901), 1 ball.

NEEDLES AND CROCHET HOOK

U.S. size 1 (2.25 mm) needles, U.S size 3 (3.25 mm) needles, U.S. size 1 steel (2 mm) crochet hook. Adjust needle size if necessary to obtain correct gauge.

NOTIONS

Stitch holder.

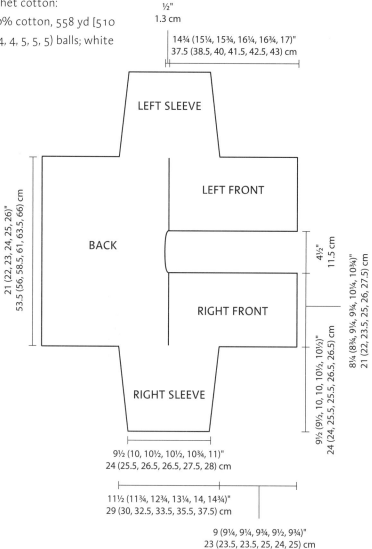

½"
1.3 cm

14¾ (15¼, 15¾, 16¼, 16¾, 17)"
37.5 (38.5, 40, 41.5, 42.5, 43) cm

LEFT SLEEVE

LEFT FRONT

21 (22, 23, 24, 25, 26)"
53.5 (56, 58.5, 61, 63.5, 66) cm

BACK

4½"
11.5 cm

RIGHT FRONT

8¼ (8¾, 9¼, 9¾, 10¼, 10¾)"
21 (22, 23.5, 25, 26, 27.5) cm

9½ (9½, 10, 10, 10½, 10½)"
24 (24, 25.5, 25.5, 26.5, 26.5) cm

RIGHT SLEEVE

9½ (10, 10½, 10½, 10¾, 11)"
24 (25.5, 26.5, 26.5, 27.5, 28) cm

11½ (11¾, 12¾, 13¼, 14, 14¾)"
29 (30, 32.5, 33.5, 35.5, 37.5) cm

9 (9¼, 9¼, 9¾, 9½, 9¾)"
23 (23.5, 23.5, 25, 24, 25) cm

GAUGE

42 stitches and 57 rows = 4" (10 cm) in stockinette stitch.

ABBREVIATIONS

See page 133.
Crochet instructions use U.S. terms, see page 133 for U.K. equivalents.

BLOUSE

Knitted sideways from Right Cuff to Left Cuff with Front Panel inserted after.

Using U.S. size 1 (2.25 mm) needles and pink, CO 100 (104, 110, 110, 114, 116) sts.
Beg with a RS row, work 4 rows in St st.
Next row K1, *k2tog, yo, rep from * to last st, k1.
Next row Purl.
Inc 1 st at each end of next row, every 14th (14th, 10th, 8th, 8th, 6th) row 3 (3, 4, 3, 14, 7) times, then every 12th (12th, 12th, 10th, 10th, 8th) row 6 (6, 7, 10, 2, 11) times— 120 (124, 134, 138, 148, 154) sts.
Work even until sleeve measures 9½ (9½, 10, 10, 10½, 10½)" (24 [24, 25.5, 25.5, 26.5, 26.5] cm), ending with a WS row. Please make a note of the number of rows worked as you will need to work the left sleeve to match.
Next row (RS) Purl.
Next row K1,* knit next st, wrapping yarn in figure 8 around both needles to make long st, rep from * to last st, k1.
Next row Purl.
Next row Knit.

Shape Right Front Body

Next row (RS) CO 95 (97, 98, 102, 101, 102) sts at beg of row, knit these sts, then knit 60 (62, 67, 69, 74, 77) sts from sleeve, turn and leave rem sleeve sts on a holder.
Cont on these 155 (159, 165, 171, 175, 179) sts only.

** Beg with a WS row, work 41 (43, 47, 47, 53, 57) rows in St st, ending with a WS row.
Knit 2 rows.
Next row K1,* knit next st, wrapping yarn in figure 8 around both needles to make long st, rep from * to last st, k1.
Next row Knit.
Beg with a RS row, work 5 (5, 7, 7, 9, 9) rows in St st, ending with a RS row.
Knit 2 rows.
Next row Purl.
Next row Knit.
Rep last 4 rows once more.
Beg with a WS row, work 11 (13, 13, 15, 17, 19) rows in St st, ending with a WS row.
Knit 4 rows.
Next row Purl.
Next row K1, *[k1, p1, k1] all in next st, p3tog, rep from * to last 2 sts, k2.
Next row Purl.
Next row K1, * p3tog, [k1, p1, k1] all in next st, rep from * to last 2 sts, k2.
Next row Purl.
Next row Knit.
Beg with a RS row, work 5 rows in St st, ending with a RS row.
Knit 2 rows.
Purl 3 rows.
Beg with a RS row, work 18 (20, 20, 22, 22, 24) rows in St st, ending with a WS row.
Knit 3 rows.
Purl 3 rows.
Beg with a RS row, work 8 (8, 8, 10, 10, 10) rows in St st, ending with a WS row.
Knit 2 rows.
Next row K1,* knit next st, wrapping yarn in figure 8 around both needles to make long st, rep from * to last st, k1.
Knit 2 rows.
Purl 3 rows. ***
BO using U.S. size 3 (3.25 mm) needles.

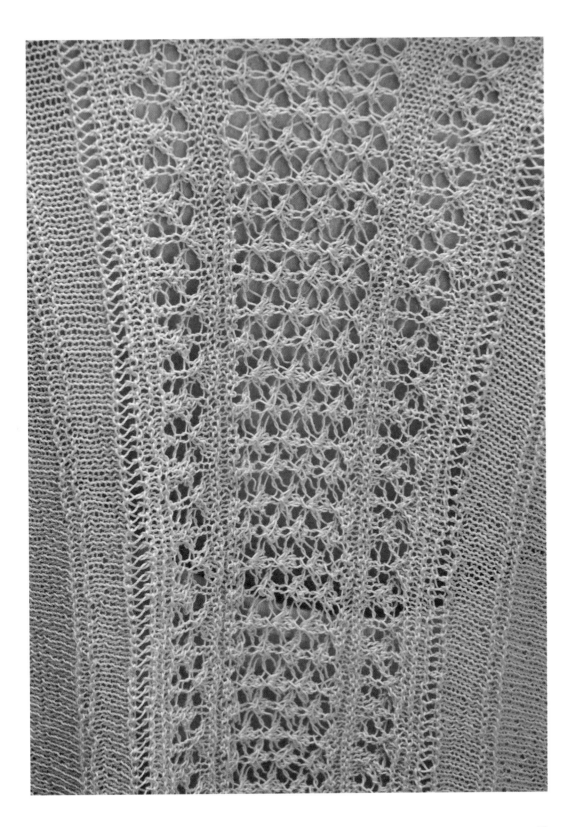

Shape Right Back Body

Return to sts on holder, rejoin yarn and using U.S. size 1 (2.25 mm) needles, knit 60 (62, 67, 69, 74, 77) sts from sleeve, then CO 95 (97, 98, 102, 101, 102) sts for Back—155 (159, 165, 171, 175, 179) sts.

Work Right Back as for Right Front from ** to ***.

Back neck shaping

Row 1 BO 4 sts, knit to end—151 (155, 161, 167, 171, 175) sts.

Row 2 Knit to last 2 sts, k2tog—1 st dec'd.

Row 3 K2tog, knit to end—149 (153, 159, 165, 169, 173) sts.

Row 4 Purl.

Row 5 K3 (2, 2, 2, 1, 3), * yo, skp, k1, k2tog, yo, k1, rep from * to last 2 (1, 1, 1, 0, 2) st(s), [yo, skp] 1 (0, 0, 0, 0, 1) time(s), k0 (1, 1, 1, 0, 0).

Row 6 Purl.

Row 7 K3 (2, 2, 2, 1, 3), * yo, k1, sk2p, k1, yo, k1, rep from * to last 2 (1, 1, 1, 0, 2) st(s), k2 (1, 1, 1, 0, 2).

Row 8 Purl.

Row 9 K3 (2, 2, 2, 1, 3), * k2tog, yo, k1, yo, skp, k1, rep from * to last 2 (1, 1, 1, 0, 2) st(s), k2 (1, 1, 1, 0, 2).

Row 10 Purl.

Row 11 K2 (1, 1, 1, 0, 2), k2tog, k1, yo, * k1, yo, k1, sk2p, k1, yo, rep from * to last 6 (5, 5, 5, 4, 6) sts, k1, yo, k1, skp, k2 (1, 1, 1, 0, 2).

Row 12 Purl.

Knit 2 rows.

Purl 2 rows.

Row 17 Knit.

Purl 2 rows.

Row 20 Knit.

Row 21 K3 (2, 2, 2, 1, 3), * k1, yo, skp, k1, k2tog, yo, rep from * to last 2 (1, 1, 1, 0, 2) st(s), k2 (1, 1, 1, 0, 2).

Row 22 P2 (1, 1, 1, 0, 2), * p1, yo, p3tog, yo, p2, rep from * to last 3 (2, 2, 2, 1, 3) st(s), p3 (2, 2, 2, 1, 3).

Row 23 Knit.

Row 24 P2 (1, 1, 1, 0, 2), * p2tog tbl, yo, p1, yo, p2tog, p1, rep from * to last 3 (2, 2, 2, 1, 3) st(s), [p2tog tbl] 1 (0, 0, 0, 0, 1) time(s), p1 (2, 2, 2, 1, 1).

Row 25 [K1, k2tog] 0 (0, 0, 0, 1, 0) time(s), k2 (1, 1, 1, 3, 2), * yo, sk2p, yo, k3, rep from * to last 3 (2, 2, 2, 1, 3) st(s), [yo, skp] 1 (0, 0, 0, 0, 1) time(s), k1 (2, 2, 2, 1, 1).

Row 26 Purl.

Rows 27 to 44 Work as given for Rows 21 to 26 3 (3, 3, 4, 4, 4) times more.

Left back neck shaping

Work in reverse order through pattern by starting at Row 20 to Row 1.

Working inc instead of dec, and CO instead of BO, work to match first side of neck.

Cont working in reverse order through to start of body, leave rem 60 (62, 67, 69, 74, 77) sts on a holder.

Left Front

Using U.S. size 1 (2.25 mm) needles, CO 155 (159, 165, 171, 175, 179) sts and work in reverse order from *** to **.

Next row (RS) BO 95 (97, 98, 102, 101, 102) sts, k60 (62, 67, 69, 74, 77), then knit across sts left on holder for left back—120 (124, 134, 138, 148, 154) sts.

Left sleeve

Beg with a RS row, work 2 rows in St st.

Next row (RS) Purl.

Next row K1,* knit next st, wrapping yarn in figure 8 around both needles to make long st, rep from * to last st, k1.

Next row Purl.

Work same number of rows even as at top of

right sleeve.

Work 1 row, ending with a WS row.

Dec 1 st at each end of next row, every 12th (12th, 12th, 10th, 10th, 8th) row 6 (6, 7, 10, 2, 11) times, then every 14th (14th, 10th, 8th, 8th, 6th) row 3 (3, 4, 3, 14, 7) times, ending with a RS row— 100 (104, 110, 110, 114, 116) sts.

Work 1 row, ending with a WS row.

Next row K1, *k2tog, yo, rep from * to last st, k1.

Next row Purl.

Beg with a RS row, work 4 rows in St st, ending with a WS row.

BO using U.S. size 3 (3.25 mm) needles.

Join shoulder seams.

Place markers 6 (6, 6, 6¼, 6¼, 6¼)" (15 [15, 15, 16, 16, 16] cm) down from shoulder on front edge.

FRONT PANEL

Faggoting and Beehive Stitch (11 sts)

Row 1 (RS) K2, yo, skp, yo, sk2p, yo, k2, yo, skp.

Row 2 K2, yo, k2tog, p3, k2, yo, k2tog.

Row 3 K2, yo, skp, k5, yo, skp.

Row 4 As Row 2.

Bead Stitch (7 sts)

Row 1 K1, k2tog, yo, k1, yo, skp, k1.

Row 2 P2tog, yo, p3, yo, p2tog.

Row 3 K1, yo, skp, k1, k2tog, yo, k1.

Row 4 P2, yo, p3tog, yo, p2.

Using U.S. size 1 (2.25 mm) needles and white, CO 53 sts.

Row 1 Sl 1, p6, work Row 1 of Bead St over next 7 sts, p7, work Row 1 of Faggoting and Beehive St over next 7 sts, p7, work Row 1 of Bead St over next 7 sts.

Row 2 K7, work 7 sts as set on Row 2 of Bead St, k7, work 11 sts as set on Row 2 of Faggoting and Beehive St, k7, work 7 sts as set on Row 2 of Bead St, k7.

These 2 rows set lace st placements and patt on all other sts, cont as set until panel fits up front edge from CO edge to marker at front neck, sewing in position at same time and ending with Row 4 of lace patts.

Split for collar.

Left Collar

Next row (RS) Sl 1, p6, work 7 sts in Bead St, p7, k2, yo, skp, k1, turn, and leave rem 27 sts on holder.

Cont on these 26 sts only.

Next row K3, yo, k2tog, k7, work 7 sts in Bead St, k7.

Rep these 2 rows until left collar fits up front edge to shoulder, ending with a WS row.

Return to sts left on holder. Leave center 1 st on holder and cont on rem 26 sts as foll:

Right Collar

Next row K3, yo, skp, p7, work 7 sts in Bead St, p7.

Next row K7, work 7 sts in Bead St, k9, yo, k2tog, k1.

Rep these 2 rows until right collar fits along front edge to shoulder, ending with a WS row.

Next row Patt across 26 sts from Right Collar, then with RS facing pick up and knit 49 (49, 49, 55, 55, 55) sts along back neck edge, then work across 26 sts from Left Collar working first st as p1, instead of sl 1— 101 (101, 101, 107, 107, 107) sts.

Next row Patt first and last 26 sts as set, knit center sts.

Next row Patt first and last 26 sts as set, purl center sts.

Work these last 2 rows until collar measures 2½" (6.5 cm) from back neck, ending with Row 4 of patt.

Next row (RS) K3, yo, skp, p7, rep 7 sts of Row 1 of Bead St to last 12 sts, p7, k2, yo, skp, k1.

Next row K3, yo, k2tog, k7, rep 7 sts of Row 2 of Bead St to last 12 sts, k9, yo, k2tog, k1.
Working edge sts as set, work Rows 3 and 4 of Bead St patt.
Next row K3, yo, skp, purl to last 5 sts, k2, yo, skp, k1.
Next row K3, yo, k2tog, knit to last 3 sts, yo, k2tog, k1.
Rep last 2 rows 2 times more.
Leave sts on a holder.

BACK LOWER BAND

With RS facing, using U.S. size 1 (2.25 mm) needles, pick up and knit 160 (164, 168, 174, 180, 186) sts along Back Lower Edge.
Next row K4, purl to last 4 sts, k4.
Next row Knit.
Rep last 2 rows until band measures 1¾" (4.5 cm), ending with a RS row.

Knit 5 rows.
BO knitwise using U.S. size 3 (3.25 mm) needles.

FRONT LOWER BAND

Work as given for Back Lower Band.

FINISHING

Sew side and underarm seams.

COLLAR EDGING

Using U.S. size 1 steel (2 mm) crochet hook and white, beg at BO edge of left front collar, sc 80 (80, 80, 84, 84, 84) down left front opening to center, dc into center st from holder, sc 80 (80, 80, 84, 84, 84) up right front opening.
Next row Ch 4, skip edge of last row, sc in live st, (ch 4, 1 sc in each of next 3 live sts) to end of collar, ch 1, sc into first sc of last row, * ch 4, skip 1 sc, sc into next 2 sc of last row, rep from * to end.

CUFF EDGING

Using U.S. size 1 steel (2 mm) crochet hook and white, sc 97 (97, 100, 100, 103, 103) around bottom edge of sleeve.
Next row Ch 1, sc into first sc of last row, *ch 4, skip 1 sc, sc into next 2 sc of last row, rep from * to end.

Openwork gloves

These finely knitted gloves look back to the 1940s and 50s, when no elegant winter outfit was complete without coordinating accessories. The openwork rose lace motif worked on the back of the hand, and the flared contrast-edged cuff, give them a pretty and unique touch. Knitted in the same lace-weight yarn as the Lace Scarf, they could be made as a color-coordinated set.

Accessories inspiration

I love the 1940s needlecraft magazines, as they often offer a great range of accessories in fine yarns using a variety of stitch textures. This picture is taken from a vintage *Stitchcraft* magazine. The lace-rib stockings on page 56 are similar to the ones shown here, and you could knit them in colors like these, to match the gloves, if you wish.

FINISHED SIZE
To fit an average sized woman's hand.

YARN
Lace-weight yarn:
Rowan "Fine Lace" (80% baby suri alpaca, 20% extra fine merino, 437 yd [400 m]/50 g): MC 20 g of purple (Era 927); CC small amount of pink (Antique 921).

NEEDLES AND CROCHET HOOK
U.S. size 2 (2.75 mm) needles; 1 set U.S. size 2 (2.75 mm) double-pointed needles (dpns); U.S. size C-2 (2.75 mm) crochet hook.
Adjust needle size if necessary to obtain correct gauge.

NOTIONS
2 small glass buttons, ½" (13 mm) diameter; sewing needle and thread (for sewing on buttons) .

GAUGE
32 stitches and 44 rows = 4" (10 cm) in stockinette stitch.

ABBREVIATIONS
See page 133.
Crochet instructions use U.S. terms, see page 133 for U.K. equivalents.

FOR BOTH HANDS
Using U.S. size 2 (2.75 mm) needles, CO 85 sts in CC.
Change to MC and cont as foll:
Row 1 (WS) Purl.
Row 2 K1, * yo, k1, sk2p, k1, yo, k1, rep from * to end.
Rep these 2 rows until 19 rows have been worked, ending with a WS row.
Next row [K2tog] across row to last st, k1—

43 sts.
Next row Purl.

FOR RIGHT HAND ONLY
Start thumb shaping
Next row K34, M1, k2, M1, k7—45 sts.
Work 3 rows even in St st.
Next row K34, M1, k4, M1, k7—47 sts.
Work 3 rows even in St st.
Next row K34, M1, k6, M1, k7—49 sts.
Work 3 rows even in St st.
Next row K34, M1, k8, M1, k7—51 sts.
Next row Purl.
Next row Knit sts onto 3 dpns as foll: 13 sts on first needle, 15 sts on second needle, and 23 sts on third needle.
Cont working in the rnd and **AT SAME TIME** work 23 rnds of lace motif pattern on 15 sts of second needle as set below, and increase sts for thumb as set (on third needle) every 4th rnd twice more—55 sts.
Work 7 more rnds without shaping then slip 14 sts of thumb gusset onto piece of yarn and leave, CO 6 sts, knit to end—47 sts.

Lace motif pattern (15 sts)
Rnd 1 K4, k2tog, [k1, yo] twice, k1, skp, k4.
Rnd 2 (thumb shaping rnd) K3, k2tog, k1, yo, k3, yo, k1, skp, k3.
Rnd 3 K2, k2tog, [k1, yo] twice, s2kp, [yo, k1] twice, skp, k2.
Rnd 4 K1, k2tog, k1, yo, k7, yo, k1, skp, k1.
Rnd 5 K2tog, k1, yo, k3, yo, s2kp, yo, k3, yo, k1, skp.
Rnd 6 (last thumb shaping rnd) Knit.
Rnd 7 As Rnd 1.
Rnd 8 As Rnd 2.
Rnd 9 As Rnd 3.
Rnd 10 As Rnd 4.
Rnd 11 As Rnd 5.
Rnd 12 Knit.

Rnd 13 K5, k2tog, yo, k1, yo, skp, k5.

Rnd 14 (thumb base rnd) K4, k2tog, yo, k3, yo, skp, k4.

Rnd 15 K3, [k2tog, yo] twice, k1, [yo, skp] twice, k3.

Rnd 16 K2, k2tog, yo, k7, yo, skp, k2.

Rnd 17 [K1, k2tog, yo] twice, k3, [yo, skp, k1] twice.

Rnd 18 Knit.

Rnd 19 K3, [yo, skp] twice, k1, [k2tog, yo] twice, k3.

Rnd 20 Knit.

Rnd 21 K4, yo, skp, yo, sk2p, yo, k2tog, yo, k4.

Rnd 22 K5, yo, skp, k1, k2tog, yo, k5.

Rnd 23 K6, yo, sk2p, yo, k6.

When pattern has been completed, cont in St st until hand measures 1¾" (4.5 cm) above thumb hole.

Index Finger

Knit to last 7 sts of rnd, slip last 14 sts worked onto spare needle, and thread all rem 33 sts onto piece of thread; last 7 sts rem unworked. Return to 14 sts and CO 3 sts for gusset— 17 sts.

Cont in rnds until finger measures 2½" (6.5 cm).

Shape top

Next rnd [K3, k2tog] 3 times, k2— 14 sts.

Next rnd Knit.

Next rnd [K2, k2tog] 3 times, k2— 11 sts. Break off yarn, thread through rem sts, and fasten off.

Middle Finger

Slip 6 sts from thread at back of hand onto needle, pick up and knit 3 sts from gusset, knit 6 sts from thread at palm of hand, CO 3 sts— 18sts.

Cont in rnds until finger measures 3" (7.5 cm).

Shape top

Next rnd [K3, k2tog] 3 times, k3— 15 sts.

Next rnd Knit.

Next rnd [K2, k2tog] 3 times, k3— 12 sts. Break off yarn, thread through rem sts and fasten off.

Ring Finger

Slip 6 sts from thread at back of hand onto needle, pick up and knit 3 sts from gusset, knit 5 sts from thread at palm of hand, CO 3 sts— 17 sts.

Cont in rnds until finger measures 2¾" (7 cm). Shape top as given for first finger.

Little Finger

Slip rem 10 sts to 2 needles and pick up and knit 3 sts from gusset— 13 sts.

Cont in rnds until finger measures 2" (5 cm).

Shape top

Next rnd [K2, k2tog] 3 times, k1— 10 sts.

Next rnd Knit.

Next rnd [K1, k2tog] 3 times, k1— 7 sts. Break off yarn, thread through rem sts, and fasten off.

Thumb

Working on 14 sts left on a holder for thumb, slip 14 sts onto 2 needles and pick up and knit 6 sts along top of thumb hole— 20 sts. Cont in rnds until thumb measures 2½" (6 cm).

Shape top

Next rnd [K3, k2tog] 4 times— 16 sts.

Next rnd Knit.

Next rnd [K2, k2tog] 4 times— 12 sts. Break off yarn, thread through rem sts, and fasten off.

LEFT HAND

Next row (start shaping thumb) K7, M1, k2, M1, k34— 45 sts.

Working a single crochet edging

1 Make a loop of yarn on crochet hook and insert hook into work one row from edge. Wrap yarn around hook and pull through a loop to make a chain. Push hook through work into next stitch and wrap yarn again.

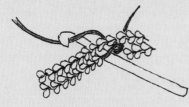

2 Two loops now on hook. Wrap yarn around hook and pull through both loops. Repeat steps 1 and 2 to form the crochet edging.

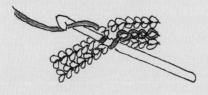

To work the button loop

3 After step 2, continue to make a chain (without inserting hook into work) to chosen length to fit button.

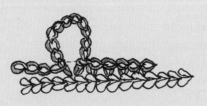

4 Insert hook back through both work and base of last chain on edging, and continue with crochet edging as in steps 1 and 2.

Work 3 rows even in St st.
Next row K7, M1, k4, M1, k34—47 sts.
Work 3 rows even in St st.
Next row K7, M1, k6, M1, k34—49 sts.
Work 3 rows even in St st.
Next row K7, M1, k8, M1, k34—51 sts.
Next row Purl.
Next row Knit sts onto 3 dpns as foll: 23 sts on first needle, 15 sts on second needle, and 13 sts on third needle.
Cont working in the rnd and **AT SAME TIME** work 23 rnds of lace motif pattern as set on right glove on 15 sts of second needle as set above, and increase sts for thumb as set (on third needle) every 4th rnd twice more—55 sts.
Work 7 more rnds without shaping then slip 14 sts of thumb gusset onto piece of yarn and leave, CO 6 sts, knit to end—47 sts.
When pattern has been completed, knit until hand measures 1¾" (4.5 cm) above thumb hole.

Index Finger

Knit 21 sts, slip last 14 sts worked onto spare needle, and thread all rem 33 sts onto piece of thread.
Return to 14 sts and CO 3 sts for gusset—17 sts.
Complete all fingers as for Right Hand.

FINISHING

Using U.S. size C-2 (2.75 mm) crochet hook, work one row sc around opening, making a small button loop at wrist.
Block and sew button in place.

Lace scarf

This frothy, lacy scarf is just the right accessory to give a tailored jacket or coat a touch of femininity. Small lacy scarves were first popular in the early 1900s, but found new favor in the 40s, too. Based on the classic Shetland shawl model of two lace patterns and an edging, this scarf, knitted in lace-weight yarn, can be worn short, as here, or could be knitted longer to make a pretty shawl.

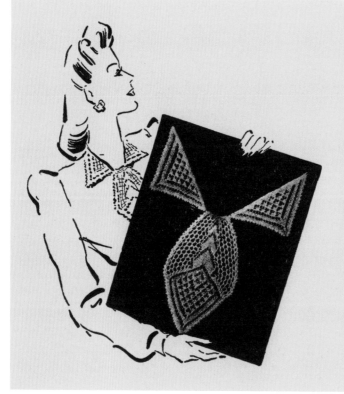

Lace scarf inspiration

A touch of knitted lace at the neck—as a kerchief, cravat, or collar—was a popular means of softening the tailored suits and dresses of the 1940s. In these times of austerity, it was also an inexpensive way to revamp an existing outfit and give it a more feminine look at the same time.

FINISHED SIZE

12½ x 27½" (32 x 70 cm).

YARN

Lace-weight yarn:
Rowan "Fine Lace" (80% baby suri alpaca, 20% extra fine merino, 437 yd [400 m]/50 g): silver (Cobweb 922), 1 ball.

NEEDLES

U.S. size 5 (3.75 mm) needles.

NOTIONS

Markers (m).

GAUGE

26 stitches and 36 rows = 4" (10 cm) in Diamond Lace Patt. Adjust needle size if necessary to obtain correct gauge.

ABBREVIATIONS

See page 133.

SCARF

CO 81 sts.
Knit 4 rows.

Spider's Web Lace

Row 1 K3, * k2tog, yo, k1, yo, k2tog, k5, rep from * to last 8 sts, k2tog, yo, k1, yo, k2tog, k3.
Row 2 K2, * k2tog, yo, k3, yo, k2tog, k3, rep from * to last 9 sts, k2tog, yo, k3, yo, k2tog, k2.
Row 3 K1, * [k2tog, yo] twice, k1, [yo, k2tog] twice, k1, rep from * to end.
Row 4 [K2tog, yo] twice, * k3, yo, k2tog, yo, k3tog, yo, k2tog, yo, rep from * to last 7 sts, k3, [yo, k2tog] twice.
Row 5 As Row 3.
Row 6 As Row 2.
Row 7 As Row 1.
Row 8 K4, * yo, sk2p, yo, k7, rep from * to last 7 sts, yo, sk2p, yo, k4.
Row 9 K3, * yo, k2tog, k1, k2tog, yo, k5, rep from * to last 8 sts, yo, k2tog, k1, k2tog, yo, k3.
Row 10 K2, * yo, k2tog, yo, sk2p, yo, k2tog, yo, k3, rep from * to last 9 sts, yo, k2tog, yo, sk2p, yo, k2tog, yo, k2.
Row 11 K1, *[yo, k2tog] twice, k1, [k2tog, yo] twice, k1, rep from * to end.
Row 12 As Row 10.
Row 13 As Row 9.
Row 14 As Row 8.
Rep Rows 1 to 14 once more.

Diamond Lace Patt

Row 1 K4, * yo, sk2p, yo, k7, rep from * to last 7 sts, yo, sk2p, yo, k4.
Row 2 K3, * k2tog, yo, k1, yo, k2tog, k5, rep from * end last 8 sts, k2tog, yo, k1, yo, k2tog, k3.
Row 3 K4, * k3, yo, k2tog, k3, k2tog, yo, rep from * to last 7 sts, k7.
Row 4 K4, * k4, yo, k2tog, k1, k2tog, yo, k1, rep from * to last 7 sts, k7.
Row 5 K4, * k5, yo, sk2p, yo, k2, rep from * to last 7 sts, k7.
Row 6 K4, * k4, k2tog, yo, k1, yo, k2tog, k1, rep from * to last 7 sts, k7.
Row 7 K4, * k3, k2tog, yo, k3, yo, k2tog, rep from * to last 7 sts, k7.
Row 8 K6, * k2tog, yo, k5, yo, k2tog, k1, rep from * to last 5 sts, k5.
Rep Rows 1 to 8 of Diamond Lace Patt until scarf measures 20" (51 cm).
Rep Rows 1 to 14 of Spider's Web Lace twice.
Work 4 rows of garter st.
BO loosely.

LACE EDGING (Make 2)

CO 9 sts. Knit 1 row.
Row 1 K3, [k2tog, yo] twice, k1, yo, k1— 10 sts.
Row 2 and every even-numbered row Knit.
Row 3 K2, [k2tog, yo] twice, k3, yo, k1— 11 sts.

Row 5 K1, [k2tog, yo] twice, k5, yo, k1—12 sts.

Row 7 K3, [yo, k2tog] twice, k1, k2tog, yo, k2tog—11 sts.

Row 9 K4, yo, k2tog, yo, sk2p, yo, k2tog—10 sts.

Row 11 K5, yo, k2tog, k1, k2tog—9 sts.

Row 12 Knit.

Rep rows 1 to 12 of Lace edging until it is long enough to fit along CO/BO edge of scarf unstretched. Block all pieces lightly and sew in place.

Lurex dress

Inspired by 1920s style, this lurex dress is knitted using a very simple, classic lace stitch that results in the striking zigzag pattern. This easy-to-knit dress, with the only shaping at the sleeves and neck, is ideal for glamorous evening wear. The dress would also look good knitted in a single color, plain yarn, and could be shortened and worn as a tunic over soft, wide palazzo pants or leggings.

Lurex dress inspiration

The style of this 1920's knitting pattern, with its simple shape, square neck, and hip-length drawstring, influenced my version, knitted in lurex yarn.

FINISHED SIZE

To fit bust 32 (34, 36, 38, 40, 42)" (81.5 [86.5, 91.5, 96.5, 101.5, 106.5] cm).
To fit hips 34 (36, 38, 40, 42, 44)" (86.5 [91.5, 96.5, 101.5, 106.5, 112] cm).
Finished length 36 (36½, 37, 37½, 38, 38½)" (91.5 [92.5, 94, 95.5, 96.5 , 98] cm).

YARN

Rowan "Shimmer" (60% cupro, 40% polyester, 191 yd [175 m]/25 g): Main (MC)—silver (Silver 092) 8 (8, 9, 9, 9, 10) balls; Contrast (CC)—dark gray (Titanium 093), 5 balls.

NEEDLES AND CROCHET HOOK

U.S. size 7 (4.5 mm) needles; U.S. size G-6 (4 mm) crochet hook. Adjust needle size if necessary to obtain correct gauge.

NOTIONS

Stitch holder; markers (m).

GAUGE

29 stitches and 25 rows = 4" (10 cm) in pattern with yarn DOUBLE.

ABBREVIATIONS

See page 133. Crochet instructions use U.S. terms, see page 133 for U.K. equivalents.

7 (7¼, 7¾, 8¼, 8½, 9)"
18 (18.5, 19.5, 21, 21.5, 23) cm

6¾ (6¾, 6¾, 7, 7, 7)"
17 (17, 17, 18, 18, 18) cm

1¾ (2, 2, 2¼, 2¼, 2½)"
4.5 (5, 5, 5.5, 5.5, 6.5) cm

1¼"
3 cm

½"
1.3 cm

6½ (7, 7, 7½, 8, 8½)"
16.5 (18, 18, 19, 20.5, 21.5) cm

FRONT AND BACK

29 (29, 29½, 29½, 29½, 29½)"
73.5 (73.5, 75, 75, 75, 75) cm

18 (18½, 19½, 20¾, 21½, 22¼)"
45.5 (47, 49.5, 52.5, 54.5, 56.5) cm

BACK

Using U.S. size 7 (4.5 mm) needles and CC yarn **DOUBLE**, CO 131 (135, 141, 151, 155, 161) sts.

Row 1 (WS) Purl.

Row 2 K1 (3, 1, 1 3, 1), *yo, k3, sk2p, k3, yo, k1, rep from * to last 0 (2, 0, 0, 2, 0) sts, k0 (2, 0, 0, 2, 0).

These 2 rows form pattern.

Working in pattern throughout cont in stripes as set below.

Rows 1 to 30 2 ends CC.

Rows 31 to 34 1 end CC and 1 end MC.

Rows 35 to 38 2 ends MC.

Rows 39 to 46 2 ends CC.

Rows 47 and 48 1 end CC and 1 end MC.

Rows 49 and 50 2 ends MC.

Rows 51 and 52 2 ends CC.

Rows 53 and 54 1 end CC and 1 end MC.

Rows 55 to 68 2 ends MC.

Rows 69 to 76 2 ends CC.

Rows 77 to 80 1 end CC and 1 end MC.

Rows 81 to 84 2 ends MC.

Rows 85 to 100 2 ends CC.

Rows 101 to 102 1 end CC and 1 end MC.

Rows 103 to 106 2 ends MC.

Rows 107 to 124 2 ends CC.

Rows 125 and 126 1 end CC and 1 end MC.

Cont in 2 ends of MC only until piece measures 27 (27, 28, 28, 28, 28)" (70 [70, 71, 71, 71, 71] cm), ending with a WS row.

Shape for sleeves

CO 2 sts at beg next 10 rows, working extra sts in pattern—151 (155, 161, 171, 175, 181) sts.

Place marker.

** Cont without shaping until armhole measures 5¾ (6¼, 6¼, 6¾, 7¼, 7¾)" (14.5 [16, 16, 17, 18.5, 19.5] cm) from marker, ending with a WS row.

Shape for neck

Next row Patt 51 (53, 56, 60, 62, 65) sts, turn, and leave rem 100 (102, 105, 111, 113, 116) sts on a holder, cont on these sts only.

Work 4 rows more on these sts, ending with a RS row.

Shape shoulder

Next row (WS) P31 (32, 34, 37, 38, 40], turn, patt to end.

Next row (WS) P11 (11, 12, 14, 14, 15), turn, patt to end.

Leave these sts on a holder.

With RS facing, working on rem sts, leave center 49 (49, 49, 51, 51, 51) sts on holder for Back Neck, rejoin yarn to rem 51 (53, 56, 60, 62, 65) sts, and patt to end.

Complete to match first side of neck reversing all shaping.

FRONT

Work as given for Back to **.

Cont without shaping until armhole measures 5¼ (5½, 5½, 5¾, 6¼, 6¾)" (13.5 [14, 14, 14.5, 16, 17] cm), ending with a WS row.

Shape neck

Next row (RS) Patt 51 (53, 56, 60, 62, 65) sts, turn, and leave rem 100 (101, 105, 111, 113, 116) sts on a holder. Cont on these sts only.

Cont without shaping until armhole matches back to start of shoulder shaping, ending with a RS row.

Shape shoulder

Work as given for Back.

Leave sts on a holder.

With RS facing, working on rem sts, leave next 49 (49, 49, 51, 51, 51) sts on holder for Front Neck, rejoin yarn to rem 51 (53, 56, 60, 62, 65) sts, and patt to end.

Complete as given for first side of neck reversing all shapings.

FINISHING

Using the three needle method, BO sts of left front shoulder and left back shoulder together.

With RS facing, using U.S. size 7 (4.5 mm) needles and MC used **DOUBLE**, pick up and knit 8 sts from right back neck, work across 49 (49, 49, 51, 51, 51) sts from back neck and **AT SAME TIME** dec 6 sts evenly, pick up and knit 8 sts from left back neck, 12 (12, 12, 14 14, 14) sts from left front neck, work across 49 (49, 49, 51, 51, 51) sts from front neck and **AT SAME TIME** dec 6 sts evenly, pick up and knit 12 (12, 12, 14, 14, 14) sts from right front neck—126 (126, 126, 134, 134, 134) sts. Purl 1 row, then BO sts.

Using the three needle method, BO sts of right front shoulder and right back shoulder together.

Join side and sleeve seams.

Using U.S. size G-6 (4 mm) crochet hook and MC used **DOUBLE**, make a ch approx 66 (70, 84, 78, 82, 86)" (167.5 [178, 188, 198, 208.5, 218.5] cm) long. Knot ends.

Crochet choker

This 1920s-inspired simple but dressy beaded crochet necklace is just the right finishing touch for a smart evening dress.

SIZE
13½" (34.5 cm).

YARN
Rowan "Shimmer" (60% cupro, 40% polyester, 191 yd [175 m]/25 g): black (Jet 095), 1 ball.

CROCHET HOOK
U.S. size B-1 (2.25 mm) crochet hook. Adjust hook size if necessary.

NOTIONS
13 x 50 mm colored glass beads
11 x 80 mm colored glass beads

SPECIAL ABBREVIATIONS
PB—slide a bead up next to hook and work 1 chain behind bead.
Crochet instructions use U.S. terms, see page 133 for U.K. equivalents.
See also page 133.

CHOKER
Ch 40, turn, slip st in 10th ch from hook (to form fastening loop), ch 112, turn, and slip st into 6th ch from hook to form loop, then work 10 sc into this loop (to start bobble fastening).

Next rnd Ch 1, 1 sc into each sc of previous rnd of bobble.
Next rnd Rep last rnd.
Next rnd (dec rnd) Ch 1, (skip 1 sc, work 1 sc) to end of rnd.
Break off yarn and pull through last st, insert bead into bobble, then use yarn end to close bobble.
First bead row Thread 13 medium beads onto yarn, then starting in ch below bobble, work slip st into next 30 ch, (ch 3, PB, ch 3, skip 2 ch and slip st into next ch, ch 7, skip 2 ch and slip st into next ch) 12 times, ch 3, PB, ch 3, skip 2 ch and slip st into next ch.
Fasten off.
Second bead row Thread 6 large beads onto yarn. Slip st through center ch of first beadless loop of first bead row, (ch 6, PB, ch 6, slip st into center ch of next beadless loop, ch 13, slip st into center ch of next beadless loop) 5 times, ch 6, PB, ch 6, slip st into center ch of last beadless loop. Fasten off.
Third bead row Thread 4 large beads onto yarn, slip st through center ch of first beadless loop of second bead row, (ch 11, PB, ch 11, slip st in center ch of next beadless loop) 4 times.
Fasten off.

Flapper dress

Inspired by the tubular designs of the 1920s, this simple shape is given drape and movement using a silky ribbon yarn. The dress is knitted in the round without shaping up to the armholes. If you prefer to draw it in at the waist, wear it with a crochet chain tie-belt threaded through the eyelets of the top row of the lace pattern. I chose to knit this one in a cherry red but it would also look good in black, to serve as the ubiquitous little black cocktail dress.

Flapper dress inspiration

This knitted dress takes its inspiration from the smart cocktail dresses worn by the "flappers" of the 1920s—fashionable young women who bobbed their hair, wore their dresses short, and enjoyed the jazz-age lifestyle.

FINISHED SIZE

To fit bust 32 (34, 36, 38, 40, 42)" (81.5 [86.5, 91.5, 96.5, 101.5, 106.5] cm).

To fit hips 34 (36, 38, 40, 42, 44)" (86.5 [91.5, 96.5, 101.5, 106.5, 112] cm).

Finished length 35½ (36, 37, 37½, 38, 38½)" (90 [91.5, 94, 95, 96.5, 98] cm).

YARN

Katia "Sevilla" (100% polyamid, 153 yd [140 m]/50 g): red (Cherry 35), 8 (9, 9, 10, 10, 10) balls

NEEDLES AND CROCHET HOOK

U.S. size 7 (4.5 mm) circular needle, 32" (80 cm) length; U.S. size G-6 (4 mm) crochet hook.

NOTIONS

Stitch holders; markers (m).

GAUGE

24 stitches and 30 rows = 4" (10 cm) in stockinette stitch.

24 stitches and 29 rows = 4" (10 cm) in lace pattern.

Adjust needle size if necessary to obtain correct gauge.

ABBREVIATIONS

See page 133. Crochet instructions use U.S. terms, see page 133 for U.K. equivalents.

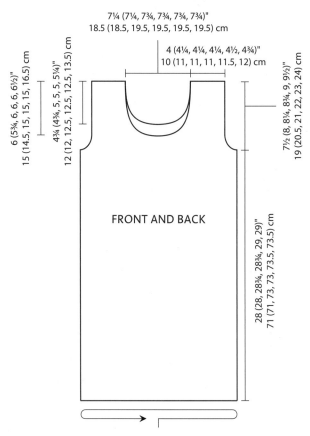

7¼ (7¼, 7¾, 7¾, 7¾, 7¾)"
18.5 (18.5, 19.5, 19.5, 19.5, 19.5) cm

4 (4¼, 4¼, 4¼, 4½, 4¾)"
10 (11, 11, 11, 11.5, 12) cm

6 (5¾, 6, 6, 6, 6½)"
15 (14.5, 15, 15, 15, 16.5) cm

4¾ (4¾, 5, 5, 5, 5¼)"
12 (12, 12.5, 12.5, 12.5, 13.5) cm

7½ (8, 8¼, 8¾, 9, 9½)"
19 (20.5, 21, 22, 23, 24) cm

FRONT AND BACK

28 (28, 28¾, 28¾, 29, 29)"
71 (71, 73, 73, 73.5, 73.5) cm

36¼ (38¾, 40¾, 42¾, 44¾, 46)"
92 (98.5, 103.5, 108.5, 113.5, 117) cm

NOTE

Due to the nature of this yarn, this garment will drop slightly in wear. When working it is best to measure your work whilst it hangs from the needles rather than laid flat.

BODY

Using U.S. size 7 (4.5mm) needles, CO 216 (232, 240, 256, 264, 272) sts.

Place marker (pm) and join for working in rnds, being careful not to twist sts.

Knit 1 rnd.

Cont as foll:

Rnd 1 * K1, yo, skp, k3, k2tog, yo, rep from * to end.

Rnd 2 and all other even-numbered rnds Knit.

Rnd 3 * K2, yo, skp, k1, k2tog, yo, k1, rep from * to end.

Rnd 5 * K1, yo, skp, yo, sk2p, yo, k2tog, yo, rep from * to end.

Rnd 7 As Rnd 3.

Rnd 9 * K3, yo, sk2p, yo, k2, rep from * to end.

Rnds 11, 13 and 15 * K1, k2tog, k1, yo, k1, yo, k1, skp, rep from * to end.

Rnd 17 As Rnd 1.

Rnd 19 As Rnd 3.

Rnd 21 As Rnd 5.

Rnd 23 As Rnd 3.

Rnd 25 As Rnd 9.

Rnd 26 Knit.

These 26 rnds set patt.

Cont in patt until piece measures 17" (43 cm) from beg, ending with Rnd 26 of patt.

Next rnd

Size 32" (81.5 cm) only

Next rnd Patt 16, (M1, k100) twice— 218 sts.

Sizes 36" (91.5 cm), 40" (101.5 cm), and 42" (106.5 cm) only

Next rnd Patt 16, (M1, k56 [62, 64]) 4 times— 244 (268, 276) sts.

Sizes 34" (86.5 cm) and 38" (96.5 cm) only

Next rnd Patt 16, knit to end.

All sizes

Next rnd Patt 16, knit to end.

Working 16 sts at center front in lace patt as set and all rem sts in St st, cont until piece measures 28 (28, 28¾, 28¾, 29, 29)" (71 [71, 73, 73, 73.5, 73.5] cm) from beg, ending with odd-numbered patt rnd.

Shape armholes

Next rnd Patt 16, k43 (46, 49, 51, 54, 56), BO next 7 (8, 8, 10, 10, 10) sts, k102 (108, 114, 118, 124, 128), BO next 7 (8, 8, 10, 10, 10) sts, k43 (46, 49, 51, 54, 56).

Front

Next row Patt 16, knit to armhole, turn, purl 102 (108, 114, 118, 124, 128). Leave rem sts on holder and cont on these sts only.

Dec 1 st at each end of next 1 (3, 5, 7, 9, 10) row(s), then every other row 4 (4, 4, 3, 3, 3) times— 92 (94, 96, 98, 100, 102) sts.

Work 3 (5, 3, 7, 7, 7) rows without shaping, ending with a WS row.

Shape for neck

Next row K38 (39, 40, 41, 42, 43), turn and leave rem 54 (55, 56, 57, 58, 59) sts on a holder.

Cont on these 38 (39, 40, 41, 42, 43) sts only.

Dec 1 st at neck edge every row 4 times, every other row 5 times, then every 4th row 5 (5, 6, 6, 6, 6) times— 24 (25, 25, 26, 27, 28) sts.

Cont without shaping until armhole measures 7½ (8, 8¼, 8¾, 9, 9½)" (19 [20.5, 21, 22, 23, 24] cm), ending with a WS row.

Leave rem sts on a holder.

With RS facing, rejoin yarn to rem front sts, BO center 16 sts, knit to end— 38 (39, 40, 41, 42, 43) sts.

Complete second side to match first side of neck, reversing all shaping.

Back

With RS facing, rejoin yarn to sts left on a holder for back, knit to end.

Cont in St st, dec 1 st at each end of next 1 (3, 5, 7, 9, 10) row(s), then every other row 4 (4, 4, 3, 3, 3) times—92 (94, 96, 98, 100, 102) sts.

Work 11 (13, 11, 15, 15, 15) rows without shaping, ending with a WS row.

Shape back neck as front neck.

FINISHING

Using the three needle method, BO sts of left front shoulder and left back shoulder together, and right front shoulder and right back shoulder together.

Using U.S. size G-6 (4 mm) crochet hook and with RS facing, work 1 row of single crochet evenly around neck and armhole edges.

Beaded purse

This little purse is inspired by the heavily beaded purses of the 1930s. They are just the thing to fit into a retro clutch bag.

FINISHED SIZE

3¼ x 2½" (8 x 6.5 cm).

YARN

Lace-weight yarn:
South West Trading "Xie" (100% bamboo, 920 yd [841 m]/100 g): teal (483), 1 cone.

NEEDLES

U.S. size 3 (3.25 mm) needles; one U.S. size 5 (3.75 mm) needle. Adjust needle size if necessary to obtain correct gauge.

NOTIONS

Approx 1400 x 2.5mm and 3.3 mm glass beads in a mixture of small silver-lined crystal and frosted amethyst, marbled marine green, dark blue lined aqua, black iris, teal lined crystal, and blue lined crystal; metal purse frame 3¼" (8 cm) wide.

GAUGE

45½ stitches = 4" (10 cm) in pattern.

BEADING NOTE

Before starting to knit, mix beads together so that colors and sizes will appear at random. Thread beads onto yarn by threading a fine sewing needle (one which will easily slip through beads) with sewing thread. Knot ends of thread and then pass end of yarn through this loop. Thread a bead onto sewing thread then gently slide it along and onto knitting yarn. Cont in this way until required number of beads are on yarn. To avoid damaging yarn whilst slipping beads along yarn, it is recommended that only 200 or so beads are threaded onto yarn at one time. Once these beads have been used up, break yarn and thread more beads onto yarn before continuing.

SPECIAL ABBREVIATIONS

bead 1—with yarn at RS of work, slip next st purlwise and slide a bead along yarn so that it sits on RS of work in front of slipped st. See also page 133.

PURSE

Using U.S. size 3 (3.25 mm) needles, CO 37 sts.

Row 1 (RS) K1, *slip next st with yarn at front (RS) of work, k1, rep from * to end.

Row 2 K1, p1, *slip next st with yarn at back (RS) of work, p1, rep from * to last st, k1.

Rows 3 and 4 As Rows 1 and 2.

Row 5 K1, slip next st with yarn at front (RS) of work, *k1, bead 1, rep from * to last 3 sts, k1, slip next st with yarn at front (RS) of work, k1.

Row 6 K1, p1, slip next st with yarn at back (RS) of work, p1, *bead 1, p1, rep from * to last 3 sts, slip next st with yarn at back (RS) of work, p1, k1.

Rep Rows 5 and 6 until purse measures 4½" (11.5 cm), ending with a WS row.

Rep Rows 1 and 2 twice.

Using a U.S. size 5 (3.75 mm) needle, BO.

FINISHING

Sew knitted section to purse frame, then sew side seams.

Practical information

The following information will help you follow the knitting patterns in this book and achieve success with your knits.

UNDERSTANDING GAUGE

Correct gauge determines the correct size of a knitted project. To make sure your project is the size you require, you must work to the gauge given at the start of each pattern, as this controls the shape and size of the knitted piece. To check your gauge, knit a square of 5" (12.5 cm) in the stitch described. Then mark the central 4" (10 cm) of the square with a pin and count the number of rows and stitches in this area. If you have the same number of rows and stitches, you are knitting to the right gauge. If you have more stitches and rows than recommended, try again using thicker needles. If you have fewer stitches and rows, try using finer needles. Once you have the correct gauge, the measurements of your piece will be the same as those in the pattern.

SIZES

If the pattern offers several sizes, the first figure is for the smallest size and those in parentheses are for larger sizes. Make sure you follow one set of figures throughout. Where there is only one set of figures given, this applies to all sizes. If a 0 (zero) or a – (hyphen) is given for your size, this instruction does not apply to your size. Follow either inch or centimeter measurements throughout.

ACHIEVING A GOOD FINISH

The manner in which you stitch your knitted pieces together is important: doing it well will give a smart, professional result. There are two stages to the process. The first is to press the pieces to the right size; the second is to stitch them together neatly and in the right order.

Pressing

To press a knitted piece correctly, lay it face down and gently stretch it out to the right length and width measurements. Then pin in position to a backing cloth (this is known as blocking). Follow the instructions on the ball band of the yarn used. If allowed, steam press the piece avoiding ribbing, garter stitch areas, and any raised stitches. Take care to press the edges, as this will make stitching simpler and much neater. If the yarn cannot be steamed, then cover the blocked-out knitted piece with a damp white cotton cloth and let stand to create the desired effect. If there are any loose ends of yarn, darn them in neatly along the selvedge edge or a color join, as appropriate.

Stitching pieces together

When stitching two knit pieces together, match any pattern or color carefully where they meet. Use backstitch or, for thicker pieces, mattress stitch (an edge to edge stitch that creates an invisible flat seam) for all main knitting seams. Ribbed areas are usually best joined with mattress stitch.

The pattern instructions normally specify the order of joining, but on garments the shoulder seams are usually joined first, then the sleeves stitched to the body, so that the center of the sleeve aligns with the shoulder seam. Join the side seams before or after the sleeves are set in.

Finally, slip stitch any pocket edgings and linings in place and sew on buttons to correspond with buttonholes. Press the seams avoiding ribbing and any areas of garter stitch.

USEFUL TIPS

Picking up bound-off stitches

To avoid unsightly holes when you pick up and knit along bound-off stitches, for example when picking up stitches at the neck of a garment, knit through both loops of the bound-off stitches, rather than just one.

Picking up dropped stitches

If you accidentally drop a stitch, it is much easier to pick the stitch up with a crochet hook. To pick up knit stitches, insert the hook into the dropped stitch, catch the bar of yarn immediately above the dropped stitch, and pull it through. To pick up purl stitches, simply turn to the knit side of the garment and use the same technique.

Joining in new yarn

Whenever possible join in new yarn at the beginning of a row, but if you have to join the yarn in the middle of a row, it pays to splice the yarn. Unravel a short length of yarn from the old ball and from the new one, and remove a strand or two from each length. Twist the strands from each ball together to make one thickness of yarn. Knit carefully through this join, trimming off any stray ends.

CROCHET ABBREVIATIONS

The simple crochet instructions in this book have been written using U.S. crochet terminology. The U.K. equivalents are as follows:

U.S.	U.K.
ch (chain)	ch (chain)
single crochet (sc)	double crochet (dc)
skip (a stitch)	miss (a stitch)

KNITTING ABBREVIATIONS

The knitting pattern abbreviations used in this book are as below:

alt	alternate
approx	approximate
beg	begin(s)(ning)
BO	bind off
CC	contrast color
cm	centimeters
CO	cast on
cont	continu(e)(ing)
dec	decreas(e)(ing)
foll	follow(s)(ing)
garter st	garter stitch (K every row)
inc	increas(e)(ing)
K	knit
k2tog	knit next 2 stitches together
m	meter(s)
MC	main color
M1	make one stitch by picking up horizontal loop before next stitch and knitting into back of it
mm	millimeters
pw	purlwise
P	purl
patt	pattern
psso	pass slipped stitch over
p2sso	pass two slipped stitches over
p2tog	purl next 2 stitches together
rem	remain(s)(ing)
rep	repeat
rev St st	reverse stockinette stitch
rnd	round(s)
RS	right side
skp	sl 1, k1, psso
sl 1	slip one stitch
st(s)	stitch(es)
St st	stockinette stitch (1 row K, 1 row P)
tbl	through back of loop(s)
tog	together
WS	wrong side
yd	yard(s)
yo	yarn over

Yarns and suppliers

YARN INFORMATION

Rowan "Siena 4-ply"
100% mercerized cotton; 50 g (153 yd/140 m) per ball.
Recommended gauge: 28 sts and 38 rows to 4" (10 cm) over St st using U.S. size 2–3 (2.75–3 mm) knitting needles.

Rowan "Fine Lace"
Lace-weight yarn
80% baby suri alpaca, 20% extra fine merino; 50 g (437 yd/400 m) per ball.
Recommended gauge: 20–39 sts and 33–54 rows to 4" (10 cm) over St st using U.S. size 0–6 (2–4 mm) knitting needles.

Rowan "Shimmer"
60% cupro, 40% polyester; 25 g (191 yd/175 m) per ball.
Recommended gauge: 29–34 sts and 36–40 rows to 4" (10 cm) over St st using U.S. size 2–3 (2.75–3.25 mm) knitting needles

DMC "Petra 5"
Size 5 pearl cotton
100% cotton; 100 g (437 yd/400 m) per ball.

DMC "Pearl Cotton no 8"
Size 8 pearl cotton
100% cotton; 10 g (95 yd/87 m) per ball.

Olympus "Emmy Grande Herbs"
Crochet cotton
100% cotton; 20 g (96 yd/88 m) per ball.

South West Trading "Xie"
100% bamboo; 100 g (920 yd/841 m) per cone.

Swans Island "Fingering"
100% organic merino wool; 100 g (580 yd/ 522 m) per skein.
Recommended gauge: 8 sts to 1" (2.5 cm) measured over St st using U.S. size 3 (3.25 mm) knitting needles.

Anchor "Freccia 20"
Size 20 crochet cotton
100% cotton; 50 g (558 yd/510 m) per ball.

Anchor "Pellicano 12"
Size 12 crochet cotton
100% mercerized crochet cotton; 50 g (421 yd/385 m) per ball.

Patons "Fairytale Dreamtime 3-ply"
100% pure new wool; 50 g (371 yd/340 m) per ball.
Recommended gauge: 32 sts and 40 rows over St st using U.S. size 2/3 (3mm) knitting needles.

Classic Elite "Silky Alpaca Lace"
70% alpaca, 30% silk; 50 g (440 yd/402 m) per ball.
Recommended gauge: 8 ½ sts to 1" (2.5 cm) over St st using U.S. size 2 (2.75 mm) knitting needles.

Katia "Sevilla"
100% polyamid; 50 g (153 yd/140 m) per ball.
Recommended gauge: 24 sts to 4" (10 cm) over St st using U.S. size 5 (3.75 mm) knitting needles.

SUPPLIERS OF YARNS AND MATERIALS

The yarns and materials in this book can be bought from the following companies:

DMC Corporation
10, Basin Drive, Suite 130
Kearny, NJ 07032
Tel: 973-589-0606
www.dmc-usa.com
for Pearl cotton and Petra crochet yarns

Westminster Fibers Inc.
165 Ledge Street, Nashua
New Hampshire 03060
Tel: 1-800-445-9276
www.westminsterfibers.com
for Rowan yarns

Emma Creation
30011 Ivy Glenn, Dr.Ste.122
Laguna Niguel, CA 92677 USA
Tel: and Fax: 949.249.8148
www.emmacreation.com
for Grande Herbe cotton yarn

Swans Island Blankets
231 Atlantic Hwy
Northport, Maine 04849
Tel: 207 338 9691
www.swansislandblankets.com
for Swans Island yarns

Coats & Clark
Consumer Services
P.O.Box 12229
Greenville, SC 29612-0229
Tel: (800) 648-1479
www.coatsandclark.com
for Anchor yarns

Classic Elite Yarns
122 Western Ave
Lowell, MA 01851- 1434
Tel: 1-978-453-2837
www.classiceliteyarns.com

South West Trading
Tel: (866) 794-1818
www.soysilk.com
for bamboo yarn

www.yarnmarket.com
for Katia yarn

Beads

Toho Seed Beads
Toho Co. Ltd
Head Office, 2-19-6, Misasa-Machi, Nishi-Ku,
Hiroshima, 733-0003 Japan
Tel: 81-82-237-5169
Fax: 81-82-537-0880
www.tohobeads.net

www.artbeads.com
sells Toho seed beads and glass fire-polished beads

www.dibeads.com
sells Toho seed beads and glass fire-polished beads

Other materials

M&J Trimming
1008 Sixth Ave
New York, NY 10018
www.mjtrim.com
silk ribbon and glass buttons

continued

www.purseparadise.com
purse frames and glass seed beads

www.emmacreation.com
variety of trimmings and yarns

www.zeldasbuttons.com
www.vintagebuttons.net
vintage buttons

OTHER ONLINE SOURCES AND INFORMATION

www.jimmybeanswool.com
stocks Rowan, Classic Elite, and Katia

www.ravelry.com
A social networking site for knitters which amongst many other things has a great search facility for finding every type of yarn available from around the world

www.etsy.com
a site selling handmade items which is also a good source for knit-related supplies

www.yarndex.com
a good yarn reference site featuring profiles of over 5,000 yarns and where to buy them

www.craftyarncouncil.com
features yarn standards and guidelines for knit and crochet, including abbreviations, yarn weights, gauges, etc.

www.vintagetextile.com
I love looking at the beautiful vintage garments and accessories for sale on this website, for inspiration

For alternative yarn ideas and any queries go to www.jennieatkinson.com

Acknowledgments

Publishers' Acknowledgments
We would like to thank the following for their help in creating this book: Nick Sargeant for photography, Anne Wilson for design, Katie Hardwicke for editing, Ana Albulescu for modelling, LIght Locations for photography locations, Sue Whiting and Sarah Hatton for pattern writing, Lisa Richardson for the charts, and Therese Chynoweth for the schematics and for pattern checking. We would also like to thank Dover Publications for permission to reproduce the images on: pp 40, 80, and 87 from *Fashions of the 30s: Selected by Carol Belanger Grafton*; p 77 from *Shoes, Hats and Accessories: A Pictorial Archive 1850– 1940*; and pp 41 and 65 from *The Mode in Costume: A Historical Survey* (R. Turner Wilcox).

Author's Acknowledgments
I would like to thank all the people who worked on this book for their valuable contribution to it. I am also grateful to Allison Korleski at Interweave Press for giving me the opportunity to create this book.

Lastly a big thank you to my dear friends Jenny and Nick Sargeant for all their encouragement and support, and especially to Nick for the beautiful photographs.